The Enlightened Soul

Wisdom from White Feather
given through the mediumship of
Robert Goodwin

*Best wishes
Robert Good-*

*Compiled and edited by
Robert & Amanda Goodwin*

The Enlightened Soul
Wisdom from White Feather

Copyright 2008 Robert & Amanda Goodwin

All rights reserved. No part of this publication may be reproduced or transmitted in any form or by any means, electronic or mechanical, including photo-copying, recording or any information storage or retrieval system, without either prior permission in writing from the publisher or a licence permitting restricted copying.

ISBN 978 0 9535210 4 3

Other White Feather publications:
Truth from the White Brotherhood
First published 1998

The Golden Thread
First published 1999
Reprinted 2005

Answers for an Enquiring Mind
First published 2002

In the presence of White Feather
First published 2005

All of the above books are available from the White Feather website:
www.whitefeather.org.uk

Email: mail@whitefeather.org.uk

Cover design: Dolphin Associates
'Stands of Time' image (page 4) taken from an original painting by Ritch Gaiti and reproduced with kind permission. www.gaiti.com

Printed in the UK

Published by R.A. Associates

In the sea of endless movement you are but a droplet,
travelling where the currents of your thoughts take you...

...that your ocean may spend a little while lapping upon these
shores fills us with delight...

...for here you have come home,
to rediscover what your soul already knows.

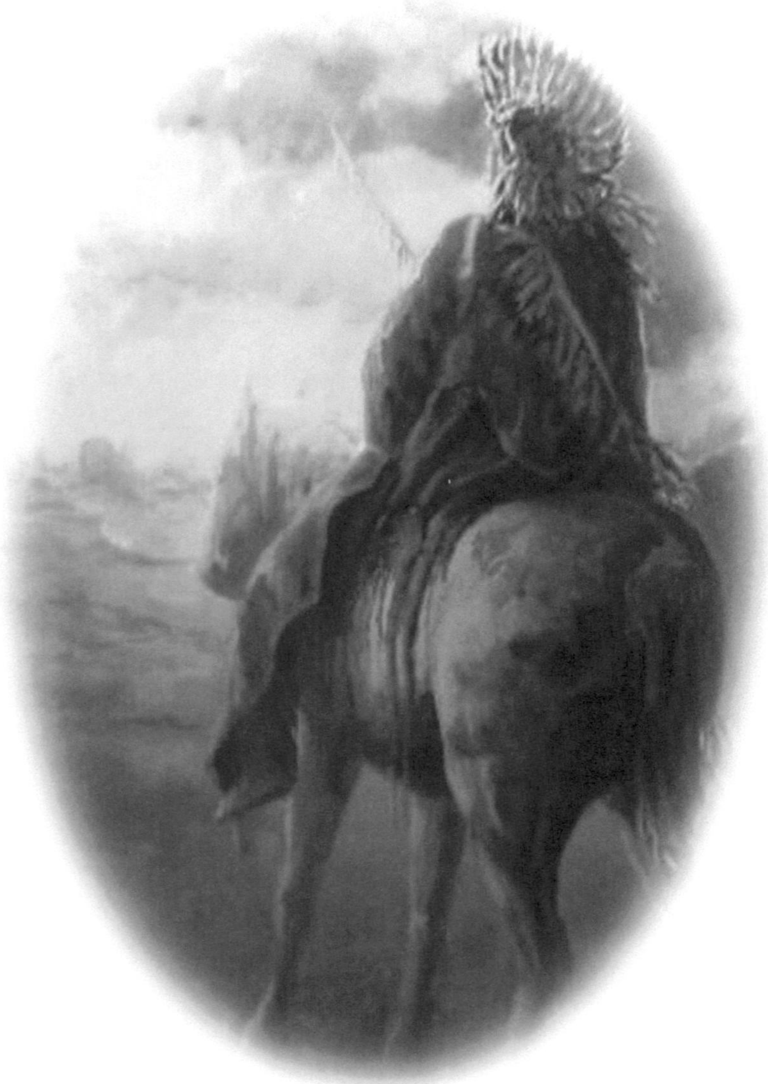

Readers should be aware that White Feather's teachings
are exclusively oral and the contents of this book have been transcribed
from recordings of his communications between 2005 - 2008.
Wherever possible the text remains
true to the spoken word despite some inevitable repetition
and only punctuation has been added in the interests of continuity.

We would like to thank all who have given their
time and energy to attend either private or public trance sittings
with us and for their enthusiasm, kindness and patience. We hope that
our editing of the original transcripts meets with your approval.
Every attempt has been made to retain the respect that you deserve
throughout this publication and any authors comments
which have been added are only for the purposes of continuity
or to further enhance readers' understanding.
Some names may have been changed to protect privacy and any
which bear a resemblance to persons living in this or the
next world are purely coincidental.

We also express our gratitude to everyone connected
with this work, particularly those who have recorded
public demonstrations on our behalf and of course
those unseen souls in the spirit realms whose
love, guidance and protection is palpable.

Without you, this book would not have been written.

The Enlightened Soul - Wisdom from White Feather

Contents

Foreword
Preface
Introduction

1. The implicit order **19**
2. The greatest drug of all **31**
3. Knowing the soul **55**
4. Amongst healers **67**
5. Resonance **101**
6. The abundant stream **113**
7. Twist of the tale **139**
8. Animal instincts **173**
9. A glimpse of the future **189**

The Enlightened Soul - Wisdom from White Feather

Foreword

Some fifty years ago I set out to discover what life is all about. Discussions with like minds began to convince me that orthodox religions could not provide the answers I sought. Though I explored their teachings and even delved into eastern mysticism, yet none provided answers to that all important question "why"?

Libraries and bookshops were searched, but only provided a woolly mumbo-jumbo that came down to the need for 'faith', a faith that defied reason, a faith that required the student to close his mind to all but the ideas provided.

Yet in our present world we are taught to question, to test ideas by rational thought. Still the powers that be wonder why it is our churches contain fewer and fewer people. Can they not see the dissatisfaction of thinking people with orthodox religion which fails to answer the burning questions of today?

As the years went by the questions remained until in time I began to realise that the answers *are* available. They come through the spirit sages whose teaching is clear and comprehensible, but always with a caveat that if what they said did not make sense then it should be set on one side; not necessarily rejected, just put away in a mental store to await the accumulation of other evidence.

So it is with the passage of time mankind has been provided with the answers to our question, answers which drop into place like pieces of a jigsaw puzzle. They do not require 'faith', only a willingness to listen and think for oneself. Thus we have the teachings of Ramadahn, White Eagle and Silver Birch over the years until today White Feather comes, still with the same caveat as before but now with answers fitted to our present problems. Answers which ring true and sound, pearls of wisdom to help us on our way through a morass which threatens to confuse and close the mind by its very complexity.

Do not despair. There is a reason for everything. "Why" is still worth asking. Maybe White Feather can provide the answers?

David Goodman
A.M. Inst. P
November 2007

Preface

In the physical universe nothing is ever still. Out in the cosmos, stars explode, new galaxies are born, worlds collide and new life forever comes into being. Much the same occurs within the inner universe, at the levels of the infinitely small.

Even in our own lives, change happens and nothing is the same today as it seemed to be, or indeed was, yesterday. Our friends, families and associates seem always to have been there, yet they too will pass, if only in the material sense, from our lives. We make our plans for tomorrow and God laughs – or so the saying goes.

Yet some things remain constant – truth for one, life itself for another. Being aligned to both, we have access to eternal existence and infinite wisdom. As the sands of life shift around and about us, this knowledge alone should provide some comfort and solace in times of doubt or despair.

White Feather, the spirit teacher whose words you are about to read is one who carries the torch of the infinite and whose philosophy has illumined the hearts and minds of many souls across the years. He is an ambassador of truth and a deliverer of information that both enlightens and uplifts the spirit. As his medium, I feel both privileged and humbled to work alongside him, as I do also my wife Amanda, whom the guide lovingly refers to as Sunflower.

At the time of compiling this fifth book of spiritual philosophy it is becoming ever more obvious to me that a darker agenda is being forcibly imposed upon the majority of people living upon planet earth. Quite who is behind this I know not, but like many others I sense a time of foreboding ahead, with freedom and liberty being replaced by covert control and manipulation. The seeds are being sown right now and their fruit is a bitter one for all to swallow.

It is at times such as this that the inspirational words of guides like White Feather are needed most. As the teacher himself has been heard to say 'if one soul can be touched, then our work has been worthwhile'.

It is my sincere wish that more than *one* soul reading these words will be touched at the deepest level. For if the world is to change for the better and if the current downward spiral is to be reversed, awakened souls need to come forth and be heard. I can only trust that the information that has been given through me for over thirty years proves to be correct. At the core of this teaching is a message that shouts out 'light is greater than darkness'. I know this to be right. I also believe my mentor when he says that 'although man can hinder and delay, he cannot prevent the will of the Great Spirit from outworking itself'.

Whatever befalls you, do not forget this and remember always that you are an infinite being, upon an eternal pathway. You have never died, and you will never die. The materialists and manipulators can say and do what they will, but ultimately the truth will prevail, for it is part of a vast universal scheme, conceived by perfect mind and as such cannot fail to triumph.

Please enjoy this book, and remember that its entire contents has been born and compiled out of love - the greatest force in existence.

Robert Goodwin
November 2007

Introduction

I am delighted that we are able to offer you another volume of spiritual philosophy through the mediumship of my beloved husband Rob. I feel truly blessed to share my life with two very special men.

It is with great joy that I have sat in our home with guests and at public demonstrations to hear White Feather speak.

The purpose of this book is to reach out a hand to enlightened souls and to those who are teetering on the verge of a journey that will bring new meaning to their lives.

Why is it in this day and age of technological excellence, material wealth and seemingly limitless possibilities for communication, that some of the most fundamental questions of life remain unanswered by academics?

We do not seek to impose our views or to provide all the answers to our existence, but without doubt, our spirit friends offer simple, yet profound truths by means of an explanation to some of the mysteries of our human imperfections.

If we search with an open mind, a loving heart and a discerning spirit then maybe we will realise that some of the answers for the enquiring mind can be found within the pages of this book. Enjoy!

Sunflower
November 2007

"Even within disorder there is order at work"

One

The implicit order

"The truth is constant. What was true yesterday is true today and will be true tomorrow." How often we have listened to White Feather utter those profound words.
No one could ever accuse the spirit sage of inconsistency. His teachings across the years have always remained faithful and consistent with his understanding and never has he wavered from the basic tenets of his philosophy. Many years ago in the first publication to feature his communications 'Truth from the White Brotherhood' he spoke of the universe as a living entity, with a consciousness that was forever unfolding:

"The whole universe, of which your galaxy is a minute part, is conscious. Just as I have said to you in the past, that consciousness lies within every portion of your being - every cell, every molecule, every atom, so the universe itself is in a state of expanding consciousness. Your earth as a planet and those who dwell upon it have much yet to unfold."

Here in a new teaching, the guide once again returns to this theme but also introduces another dimension, an aspect he refers to as 'the implicit order'. Commencing with his usual welcoming dialogue he begins by setting the scene with a few wise words and then introduces the main theme of his talk:

White Feather: "May I enfold you in the divine embrace of the Great Spirit as we join together once more to enable the almighty power and intelligence of the infinite source to flow into your world. That we are able to assist in making it available to many who seek it is a tremendous privilege and I am fully aware that the teaching I give will reach into homes in which I have never set foot, into hearts that I have never touched and into minds that are unknown to me. That is perhaps the greatest joy, for knowing that we can touch souls and help them to awaken to the glorious truth that in reality already lies half awakened within them, fills me with delight and happiness.

As I have said before, service is the coin of the spirit. To serve is noble. To serve is divine and through these humble offerings that I present to you I know that the greatest service of all is rendered, for we serve the truth and it is truth that ultimately will be mans' salvation. It is truth that will help bring him liberation and it is the light of knowledge and understanding that will vanquish the darkness of ignorance.

Ever since the consciousness that expresses itself through all of life was able to reach the point where, through human form it was able to think and reason, man has asked questions of his origins. He has pondered, he has wondered, he has weighed up and considered from whence he cometh and the nature and ultimate destination of his journey. From his musings have arisen many disciplines and beliefs, with the scientific body of evidence revealing facts and information about his world and the universe and varying religious beliefs from which he has drawn a few crumbs of spiritual comfort.

Whatever your beliefs and ideas about creation – whether you adhere to Darwinism which speaks of the transmigration of species through the survival of the fittest or the more recent concept of 'intelligent design' with its leanings towards ancient scriptures, I think you will agree that there has been change across the centuries of time and that within this change there has also been evolution. For it is difficult to dispute that there were once creatures upon your world that no longer inhabit it. The fossil remains of dinosaurs and creatures long since extinct, bear this out. Even today, species are changing. Due to environmental conditions some are becoming extinct and others hang by a thread to their material life as a collective. Even man is changing and is not the same today as he was perhaps a century or more ago. Some changes are very notable and striking whilst others are more subtle.

What I want to highlight in this teaching is not merely the physical aspect of change, but the deeper *spiritual implication* behind it. For there is what I term an 'implicit order' that is infused into every aspect of creation, whether animate or inanimate, complex or simple, and it is this directive that motivates and brings life forward from lower states to higher states. You will find, if you consider creation around you and indeed, your own life, that there is an inner desire for betterment. Always there is a seeking for fulfilment. In the case of thinking, reasoning humankind, there is an unquenchable thirst to know and understand, to be one with the divine source, whatever that is perceived to be. You will find that this driving force and energy is present in everything that is.

Consider for a moment the work of a lesser creature; have you ever stopped to look at nature and watch the workings of the bee as it flits from flower to flower, gathering nectar? It is ceaseless in its pursuit in order to return to its source and fulfil its purpose. This it does perfectly, for it is not distracted by outside influences and like many things within nature, obeys implicitly its inner directive and instinctive drives. If we look at another creature, which is slightly higher in the evolutionary chain - the salmon, which having been spawned and ventured on a journey through the oceans of your world, is compelled by it knows not what, to return to the very source that gave it birth. Against overwhelming odds it struggles upstream, fighting both the onrushing current and in some instances, creatures that would wish to take away its life, eventually to reach the very same pool of water where it spawns and gives forth its physical existence.

Now you may say, observing this creature alone, that it has failed and that its death is somehow the result of its strenuous efforts, in a kind of self defeating way. Yet I say to you that it has not failed, but fulfilled its purpose and the implicit order of which it is a part. You will find if you look at every aspect of life from the lowest to the highest, from the most minute to the mightiest, that life is evolving and moving inexorably towards a higher state of consciousness."

Seeking to further emphasise his point, the sage continued by turning his attention to the inner realm of nature - the quantum world of the atom and weaves a story that highlights a particular journey and cycle that, over time must surely have occurred repeatedly:

"If we consider the humble atom and its component particles, of which man has discovered but a few, you will find that even here through the operation of natural law in which fate, luck and chance are non-existent, there is perfect order and purpose. What then - you might say, does the atom aspire to? The atom, which in essence is energy as are all things, has within it intelligence and a degree of consciousness that is part of the Great Spirit. For the atom to exist there has to be a directive within it that far transcends the laws of attraction that operate within the physical domain. Let us consider one possibility within the life of an atom; let us consider one or more atoms being part of a star in some far distant galaxy - that having fulfilled its existence over many aeons of time explodes and scatters its debris throughout the cosmos. Perhaps a group of atoms find themselves within an aspect of this star that becomes a meteorite, speeding across the vastness of space. It travels for many thousands of light years until it enters your solar system. As is passes your sun, its fiery tale burning brightly behind it, this rock composed of many elements and minerals, begins to heat. It enters the atmosphere of the earth and hits the surface creating an enormous crater. The atoms that once existed within the star from far, far away, are now within your earth and are absorbed into the soil. Over time as the landscape alters and vegetation begins to emerge, these minute forms of life are taken within a tree. They become part of a tree. They do not know they are part of a tree, because the consciousness and spirit expressing through them is not able to inform of this and yet there are the rudiments of something greater within each atom. Over time as the tree grows and it is subject to the various conditions of your world, some of its leaves are consumed by creatures who roam the earth at that time. So the atom that was once in the star and the tree, finds itself absorbed into a living, breathing creature. The creature lives its physical life, death occurs to the physical body, which decays and is absorbed again into

the earth as part of one of many, countless recurring cycles. No energy is ever destroyed or lost - it only changes from one state to another. Eventually over many thousands or perhaps millions of years, the energy that was once in the distant star or galaxy is absorbed into nutrients, finds its way into the food chain and is consumed by a new species that has evolved upon the earth – a thinking, reasoning higher intelligence called man. The atom finds its way into the DNA of that human. For the atom, this is a promotion of sorts, for here it is in a more highly refined vessel and its interactions as part of the DNA chain enable it to obtain a higher expression. It senses consciousness. It has an interaction with thought processes and deeper intelligence.
So you see what I am driving at here? You see the pattern that is emerging? Within everything that is, there is an implicit order that seeks to unfold from the lower to the higher. Because man is part of the Great Spirit which is perfection, that aspect, that facet which is manifesting through an individual or even mankind as a collective, seeks to unfold and express its latent divinity through raising the consciousness, though bringing the individual and the race into a full awareness of all that it is."

White Feather went on to reiterate that even when certain groups or individuals succumb to their lower, base instincts and drives, allowing their egos to dominate, the same spiritual force was still at work, seeking ever to manifest through life at every opportunity:

"Have you ever had the experience of walking down a street? Because your mind is perhaps at peace, aware of the gentle breeze or the birdsong and the contours of nature, you have a momentary sensation of bliss. It is as if your heart soars to something more grand and beautiful. It may last for a moment, it may last for several minutes or even longer than that and at this time it is as if a doorway has opened unto a higher self and you glimpse the divine that lies at the heart of your being. If you are honest with yourselves, each of you, you want happiness, you want peace, you want contentment – these are all part of the very same order of which I am speaking. They are part of the divine aspect that is your true self and even in those individuals that commit atrocity against other life forms, who allow their lower ego state to dictate their thoughts and their actions and motives, the same force still seeks to operate. In some it becomes diverted by the lower ego and channelled into selfishness, greed and sometimes aggression and violent behaviour. This is a distortion, but within this the principle still struggles for expression and when a breakthrough is made, at whatever point in the life history of that individual, the radiant light of truth and love can shine.

Here you will see the higher aspiration of selflessness, kindness, peacefulness, gentleness and love will begin to emerge and the higher self can express itself through all thought and word and deed. So try to understand if you can that this implicit order that is found in everything that exists is part of the divine intelligence that seeks to direct all of its creation to higher states of knowingness and perfection. There is none in whom it is not present. Even the lowest of the low whose lives are blighted by ignorance and darkness still have the divine spark within and it is this supreme force and power that will ultimately liberate and set them free from all that now binds them to the cycles of life and death – the worlds of illusion and darkness.

Remember my friends that at whatever stage you find yourself – whatever place and whatever time, that always there will be something deep within you seeking to drive you forward and bring you into the light. You may deny it, you may turn your back upon it, you may pretend it doesn't exist or that your ears cannot hear its promptings, but it will never go away. Ultimately, you can hinder, you can delay – individually and collectively as a race, but you cannot prevent the fulfilment of the divine.

As I have said before – spirit is master, matter is servant. Spirit works through matter, which is imperfect, but even within imperfection, there is perfection at work because the law cannot be cheated or abrogated and has to fulfil itself in its outworking. Form comes and goes, it changes, it alters and moves, it has many expressions, but within it is the supreme constant that is the implicit order which is part of the creative intelligence that some call God and that I refer to as the Great Spirit. The seeds have been sown and continue to be sown, but all will be gathered in and the harvest of truth and light will be known and seen and realised."

As the session came to a close it was once again evident that the spirit visitor had taken a somewhat complex teaching and delivered it in a simple fashion that all would understand - the true mark of an evolved soul. In times of difficulty, when it seems that we are surrounded by the darkness of ignorance, perhaps we may draw some comfort from his wise counsel and remember that the directing force of the infinite intelligence ever abides within, seeking always to steer its creation towards the true goal of spiritual union and ultimate freedom.

At the time of compiling this book and a week or so after White Feather had imparted the teaching contained in this chapter, scientists revealed that a massive star around 150 times the size of our own sun had exploded, creating the brightest supernova ever seen by mankind. Supernovae of this kind occur when huge, mature stars effectively run out of fuel and collapse in on themselves.

The blast, which occurred 240 million light years away, polluted the surrounding environment with the metals and elements that are needed for life and sent material soaring throughout the galaxy. Astronomers say a star in our own Milky Way system could soon be about to perform the same celestial fireworks - further evidence that the infinite process of creation continues and the implicit order forever unfolds.

"You cannot serve two masters"

Two
The greatest drug of all

Becoming addicted to mind-altering substances can be a traumatic experience for both the addict and those with whom they share their life. Drugs of all descriptions are one of the scourges of modern society and their impact is witnessed in many areas of existence, with broken homes and shattered lives often resulting from many years of abuse.

When Pauline brought along her son Paul for a specially arranged session with White Feather, the intention was for the guide to try and reach out from the afterlife to touch the soul of this young man in an attempt to both heal and advise.

Here we can witness the wise sage at his absolute best and as the sitting unravels it soon becomes evident that right from the start, whilst appearing to address the group, the guide is actually speaking directly to him, using clever language patterns with embedded messages directed to his deeper unconscious mind. It is likely that only trained therapists would recognise this technique and full credit must go to the spirit *ambassador for his approach and forethought, as no prior requests or instructions had been imparted to him. It is for this reason that we have included the transcript in its entirety even though parts of the sitting include questions of a more general nature, as an overview of the session will clearly reveal how insightful the guide had been:*

White Feather: "May I greet you all with my customary greeting and pay tribute to the operation of natural law that enables me to link with you. Excuse my momentary hesitancy but I have to ensure that all precautions have been taken and all safeguards are in place. For there are many who link with me and stand by my side as I address you this night.

I know that you and I Sunflower, have spoken many times and that there are others amongst us with whom I have shared this linking of spirit and spirit. But I welcome all who are present here and that includes many in my world who join us, as is so often the case on these occasions.

Let me say for the purposes of this evening, which I know is being recorded upon your machine, that I am like you, human. I am not special, I am not a God or a deity, I am not supernatural. I am just as you – I have human traits, frailties, weaknesses and like you I have a great deal to learn. But I hope that in some small measure I can impart to you the benefit of a deeper understanding that I have acquired and which enables me to link to a deeper pool of knowledge and higher minds even than mine, who have a greater experience to share with you.

I know that there is an eagerness to ask questions but I want to just begin by saying a few words as I like to do and I don't intend to bore you! I just want to impart something that is of interest. For you know, all knowledge, all truth, all wisdom is helpful to the individual, along their pathway. For you have many problems, many difficulties with which to contend, but if you can add to your armoury of experience the wealth of understanding and wisdom that is your true divine heritage and bring it into play in your everyday lives, then that indeed will enhance your own pathway and also those who come into your orbit to whom you can give the benefit of your illumination and shine a little light into their lives.

You know, the mention of the word 'discipline' is one that sometimes frightens people. It scares them off because it has connotations with difficulty, with the sacrifice of certain activities and with the adherence to other activities which may require strength and patience and tolerance and all manner of actions, both mental and physical, on behalf of the individual. Yet this need not be the case, because true discipline if it is practiced in earnest, brings a richness, brings a beauty, brings an unfoldment to the individual that is beyond description.

There are several types of discipline; I want to speak briefly of self-discipline. What do we mean by 'discipline'? Do you know from where the word is derived Sunflower? What is contained within the word? - spell it out in your mind."

Pauline: "Disciple."

White Feather: "Absolutely – disciple. We speak now not in a biblical sense at all, not in a religious context, but what is a disciple? A disciple is a follower of something or other. One can be a disciple of music, a disciple of philosophy, one could be a disciple of football, one could be a disciple of motor cars - a disciple of anything that requires that the individual has an understanding and intent, a desire on their behalf to follow a certain pathway of expression, often to the exclusion of other things, because it means so much to them. This is why those who were referred to in the biblical sense were called disciples – they were followers. But you know my thoughts on religion and I am not going to go down that particular pathway.

To be a disciple of spiritual development is a wonderful thing because it necessarily leads one to discipline oneself. Now when we speak of discipline, this does not need to have any negative connotations whatsoever. By true spiritual discipline, we mean adhering to certain practices and thought patterns and belief systems that allow the individual to open up their higher self and rise above the lower material form and the lower material body and brain that so often gets sucked in to materialistic actions and thoughts. Even though in the early stages of self-discipline it might require a certain degree of withdrawal and adherence to practices that might at first be difficult I can say to you all with great assurance that there will come a point where it is so easy because it has become embedded within the self, it has become a way of thinking, a way of action, a way of being and the difficult becomes easy, the complex becomes simple. This pathway of self-discipline is one that will lead you to enlightenment and will bring to you gifts which you already have and enable you to open them and use them - the gifts of spiritual vision, the gifts of healing, the gifts of clear-seeing and clear-hearing, the gifts of philosophy, the gifts of love. These things are spiritual in nature but you will not have them handed to you on a plate, you will have had to have earned them and any future things that come to you – you have to earn them. If you are undisciplined, if your only concerns are for *yourself*, for *your* world, for *your* temporary states of happiness which do not endure for very long, but come and go like the wind……they come, they stay, they pass very swiftly - if your only pleasure is in earthly things, then you have many lessons to learn. These things will not assist you in your psychic or spiritual development. If however, you have the presence of being to just stop and think, even in the crowd, even in the hubbub of life, wherever you are and you can find that inner stillness and just withdraw for a few moments, then you are linking with your higher self and you are instilling a discipline that will last you into your future progress. I cannot explain to you, I cannot stress enough how important it is that you discipline yourself and enable your higher self to have the same access to your consciousness as your lower ego mind.

When I look at all the wars in your world, all of the aggravation, all the anger, all the fear, all of this which holds man to this planet then I sometimes despair because man gets locked in to this material world. He thinks that it is reality but it is not. It is transient, it is an illusion. If only he could see beyond that he would see the rich vein of spirituality that runs through his whole being. He has only to tap into it and to enable it to come to the surface of his consciousness and he *can* do this, *you* can do this with a little time, a little patience with yourself.

Now what of the discipline of others? Sometimes…..and I know that you each have experience of this, it is necessary to discipline others, because when others are undisciplined it impacts upon your lives, your environment, your health…..all of these things. So it is not always a negative thing to impose a healthy discipline. Sometimes you have to say things and do things that seem harsh to others, but when you act from your higher standpoint, from your greater self, your higher mind, you do so in love and wisdom and if you follow your instinct you will find that it will not let you down, it will guide you perfectly.

So discipline is an important word I feel, in life. If we can learn to harness it and use it in a positive sense it is one of the most wonderful words in your language and carries with it a potency that can bring true richness to so many. Do you understand that?"

Having cleverly set the scene and sown a few seeds through his introductory talk White Feather invited those present to begin their questioning of him:

White Feather: "Now, let us commence upon our questioning. As I always say; I do not have the answers to everything under the sun, because like you I have a great deal yet to unfold and learn, but I do have access to my own experiences and those who stand by my side and if it falls within the orbit of my understanding then I will do my best to answer."

Amanda: "It is an honour as always, for us to speak to you again White Feather."

White Feather: "But not as honoured as I am to be in your presence, because there is no greater honour for me, from my side of life, to speak to you and enjoy such discussions as this."

Pauline: "When I sit on occasions like tonight and sometimes on my own in meditation, I sometimes see a kind of white mist floating around me in the room and I wondered what this is?"

White Feather: "It is ectoplasm."

Pauline: *"It is very faint, almost like smoke."*

White Feather: "It is like a swiftly moving mist. It is ectoplasm, which if you don't mind me saying, we have borrowed from each of you, taking a little bit from you [Paul] a little bit from you [Pauline] and a little from you Sunflower [Amanda] and also a little from the medium as well - because ectoplasm is not a physical substance, it is not a spiritual substance purely, it is kind of in-between – a protoplasm that you each have, some more in abundance than others. We use it as a form of energy to assist in the communication and the development of mediumship. We take it from the carpet, from the curtains, to add a little colour sometimes and in the physical circle, which I know you are beginning to look into, you will find that where there is true development of physical mediumship, ectoplasm can be used to great effect to enable the spirit form to appear before you in the room. Ectoplasm can be made to be very solid, as solid as a rock or it can be fluid. It can be like cheesecloth, it can be like water, it can take on any appearance that we choose to make."

Amanda: "Are there any things that are necessary for those who sit in a physical development circle?"

White Feather: "Yes – discipline."

Amanda: "Also, I assume, a blending of like minded people who are sitting with the honourable intent and the right motive?"

White Feather: "Yes, yes. I think the important thing is to make the choice. Once the intent and the choice has been made to sit for a particular form of development then certain criteria begin to be put into place. You have to sit with the same intent, with the same people at the same time, but not to sit for 'this' one week and 'that' another, because how do we know then what is to be agreed upon?"

Amanda: *"So if we've decided to sit for physical phenomena then it is best that we should continue to sit each week for the same thing really?"*

White Feather: "It is yes, but let me say also Sunflower, there is another part of the equation – whether those assembled have the capacity to enable physical mediumship to take place. You may get limited results and a limited response – we may have other plans for you that may involve linking with those who are still shall I say, attached to the earth and the lower planes, so that has still to be determined. You must understand - and I won't labour this point too much, but when a group get together and dedicate themselves to meeting on a regular basis to undertake spiritual work, we have to weigh up, ponder and consider all of the elements that go to make up those sitters – what their capacity and capability is to do a particular work. If it is not to be one thing then it may well be that another can transpire."

Pauline: *"What can I do to help my own development, as I sometimes find it difficult to get anything and I feel that I'm not getting anywhere?"*

White Feather: "Well, let me say it's important that you don't fall asleep [laughter from Pauline] because if you fall asleep we can do very little!"

Pauline: "I know!"

White Feather: "The mind has to be passive and yet alert, which is almost a contradiction of terms, but if you have the desire and the intent to develop then there are many things in actual fact that you can all do to enhance your development; try to learn as much as you can. Absorb, watch, observe, look at others. As I so often say; look at the fool, he will teach you much, listen to the ignorant, they may be a great teacher for you, look at the wise man, listen to that which is silent - it will speak to you, look at that which is still and see the movement within it. Read books, listen to what others speak of, all of these things – and then think upon them, ponder upon them, go within them and want to know more, want to learn. Have the desire to learn and then when it comes to the actual point where you are in a position to meditate or sit in the quiet, just lift your thoughts above the mundane, put that aside, put all fear and trepidation aside and realise that you have your own self-protection by your intent. Provided you are sensible, provided you don't dabble in areas of life that can open you up to the astral planes, provided your motive and desire is to unfold and touch the very highest, then you will find that this affords you a protection. At these times we will draw close to you.

You may get various physical feelings – a tightness in the throat, the heart beats, the head is locked, the hands cannot move, you feel hot, you feel cold, you feel a cold draught, your head is expanding……all of these things that are perfectly natural because it means that we are touching your auric field and here we can begin, though linking our channel, our stream with yours, to begin to impose our mind and our thoughts upon yours and so turn your thinking into a more spiritual river of understanding.

But again, to reiterate – if you sit regularly, if you sit with intent and with love then you will find that over a period of time….. and it's not a race, you will begin to move forward. Does that help you?"

Pauline: "Yes it does thank you. I very often find when I sit in meditation that I experience these kinds of feelings and I sometimes feel as if my head is going to explode?"

White Feather: "Well, it won't explode! – because energy, as I have said, is being drawn from you all. Energy is being taken, with your permission by the way! I didn't ask you personally but at the deeper level, at the higher level you have given permission. Let me say to you all that you would not be here tonight were it not meant to be and had you not been vetted earlier to be here. There is a purpose for it."

Up until this point Paul had been sitting very still, seemingly taking in the conversation between his mother, Amanda and the guide without saying a word. Sensing that it was time for him to join in the conversation with the other-worldly visitor he spoke to the guide in a hesitant voice:

Paul: "I'd like to ask a question, but I can't think what to ask! Before I came here tonight there were so many questions that I wanted to ask, but now I can't think what to say."

White Feather: "I think perhaps you have many questions but not enough words to put them together."

Paul: "Yes......I just have so many things in my head, so much that I wanted to talk about...."

White Feather: "Hmmm....then what puzzles you?"

Paul: "I'm curious....I do believe that there are guides and stuff like that. I've never worried about things like ghosts and spirits and things and I understand what they are. I've never disbelieved, I've always believed from the start really that there's more to life, do you know what I mean?"

White Feather: "Absolutely. Well, let me ask you a question then son; where do you think I am at the moment? Where do you think the spirit world is? Have you any idea?"

Paul: "All around."

White Feather: "All around, and all within. In fact every level of the spirit world is here now – in this room, within your body, in your mind, it is all here. If I use the age old analogy of tuning in a wireless set then perhaps you begin to get the picture then. You attune to a particular channel. Where do the other channels go? They are still there aren't they? It's a question of attuning and when the physical body dies you are in the spirit body that you have now and you will be on that frequency. The physical world will be on the same frequency but you will have moved up to a higher one and so this earthly world will be 'dead' to you, it won't exist unless you are able to tune back into it and visit those whom you left behind."

Paul: "When I die and like you say, my spirit goes to a higher place, how will my spirit change and how will appear in the spirit world - where will I be?"

White Feather: "It's a question of spiritual development. You see, if you die tomorrow son – which you won't, because you've got a little way to go yet, but if you die tomorrow *you* will still be *you*. You will still be the same individual with the same personality, but your essence, your consciousness, instead of being seated in the physical brain and physical body, will be seated in the spirit body, the astral body. The physical drops away – it is rather like peeling away the layers of an onion or an orange and you will be then at that frequency.

Now you may say to me 'well what frequency is that?' because there are many levels in my world. The level at which you find yourself when you die will be in direct accordance with the way you have fashioned and lived your life. If you have lived a selfish life and thought only of yourself, not cared about what happens to others, trampled upon others and lived for this world alone, then you will be on a lower level in my world than one who has given love and service and kindness and thought about others and tried to help them because they will have enriched and quickened their vibrations and the very molecules, atoms and particles of their spirit body will have been refined. So they will be able to manifest on a higher plane in my world – a more beautiful level. That is not a question of discrimination by God. God doesn't choose one over another, it is a self-regulatory law that operates in accordance with the actions, thoughts and deeds of every individual. Do you understand that?"

Paul: "So what you are saying is that those who have basically dedicated their lives to helping others will be better off in the spirit world?"

White Feather: "Yes, yes."

Paul: "Is heaven at the top and hell at the bottom?"

White Feather: "It's not quite as black and white as that. First of all son, there is no 'hell' as such, but there are lower levels and there are higher ascending levels. Now, no one is asking you to be a saint – whatever that is. No-one is asking you to be perfect and to be so afraid of making mistakes that you do not undertake anything. We are all human and we all err, we all make mistakes, we all stumble and fall. The point is this; if you earnestly try your best, if you give of whatever you have - and some may be able to give far more than others - but if you as individuals give of what you have and honestly do your best, that is all that can be asked of you.

You know, there are many highly evolved souls in my world who have not had any acclaim upon the earth, who have not had any recognition, who are not famous, who have worked or laboured in the field, who may even be illiterate and yet who have touched the lives of others in a simple, yet profound way because they gave of themselves. That is what spirituality is.

So, you all have that potential. You all have that choice. There is no heaven and no hell as such, it is a matter of degree. There are planes of great beauty, there are planes of darkness and it is for you to decide to which level you will pass when death occurs. In that regard you know, you cannot afford to think and act negatively – any of you. I speak to all of you, including the one through whom I am speaking tonight!"

With the spirit guide beginning to strike up a rapport with the youngster, more personal questions were beginning to flow from Paul's mind enabling the teacher to deliver his deeper message:

Paul: "Can you tell me what I am going to do in two years time? Do you have the ability to see into the future?"

White Feather: "We have the capacity to see certain events that are determined upon the pathway, because you must recognise that there are certain parameters that are set out before you come into the physical body. These are known by the soul. However, you have free will and you can change to an extent through your thoughts and actions, what befalls you on the pathway. To give you an extreme – if you decide when you leave here, to throw yourself off a bridge, then this will take your physical life from you and that will be a matter for your own free will choice. However, that may not have been on your pathway, but a matter that you decided. So you have a certain free will that comes into play and you can determine to an extent, your pathway.

There are challenges ahead for you, let me say that. What you decide now, over the next few months and years – and I am talking now of the period of eighteen months to three years, will determine to a great extent what happens to you later in life. You have reached a sort of crossroads. One of the reasons that you have come here tonight and of which you are not fully aware of yet is that there are certain truths being made available to you. It is not by accident that you and I have met. It is not by accident that this little gathering has come to be. So there is an opportunity Paul, being presented to you here; it is whether you decide to take it on board or ignore it. That is for you to decide, for your free will. If you had gone through life without being made aware of these facts, of the way that your will, your actions, your thoughts determine your spiritual and material pathway and if you did not come to the point where these opportunities were pointed out to you, then you could perhaps rightly, justifiably turn to the Great Spirit at some point and say 'I didn't know that, no-one told me that! I just came upon the earth and I had to make do with my lot! I had to do what I did because that's the way I am!' But the point is, *you are not just the way you are.* You are the way you are because of the way you have made yourself, all of you. You can change your behaviour if you want to.

You have to take a bigger view Paul. Look at the greater picture, not just a momentary fleeting happiness, a momentary joy from this pleasure or that. Look at the greater picture, and what I am saying to you is that at this moment in time the crossroads at which you are standing is offering you opportunities, but we cannot and will not force them upon you or make you take a particular road. That is for you to decide.

What you do now determines what will happen later in life because the path you walk, all of you, is the path that you have created – no one else. You are here right now, in this body at this moment in time because of what you did yesterday and the day before and the day before that, going back even to past lives. You cannot be other than where you are meant to be. So if you for example son, wanted to be a great medium or a great teacher, if you wanted to be a father, if you wanted to be a philosopher, if you wanted to be a great soul, it won't just come to you, you have to bring it into being. You have to start with that first step."

Pauline [to Paul]: "You have tried more than once haven't you, to change yourself and to come off the drugs?"

Paul: "I have come off them a few times, but it was really hard. Some time ago, I wouldn't say I hit rock bottom, but my life could have been a lot better. I lost my bearings. I had a couple of jobs, one of them a driving job, but I lost both of them because I crashed my car, I got into debt as well. I've always tried to be good, but at that time drugs were my life and in a way they still are. I'm still fighting."

Amanda: "What are you fighting?"

Paul: "Temptation. The want to do it and the want to get off them all."

White Feather: "You know son, the greatest drug of all is the drug of truth and knowledge because once you get hooked on that, then you want more. You know there is a great feeling son, of having a sense of presence in the midst of others, that you have a knowledge and a wisdom – an understanding that they do not. It is not a question of arrogance or a feeling of being better than they are, it is a question of feeling good. That you know something and have acquired a state of being that they perhaps have yet to experience and you want to help them with it. It is the greatest drug of all. The more that you have, the more that you want it and once you switch on to that energy, it is a wondrous, wondrous power."

Knowing that he was making some headway, the sage delivered a simple, yet profound metaphor before continuing to press home his philosophy that there were choices available:

"You know, a man can look at a dandelion and think that it is a weed. He can trample on it. He can pick it up and throw it in the bin or another man can look at it and see its beauty and pick it and put it in a vase to admire it. The difference is in being able to ascertain, to look with the eyes of the spirit. If you focus on material drugs, materialism – anything that feeds the lower self, then that is what you will be attracted to. That is what you will seek and desire, because you are sowing the seeds of that. What you sow has to be reaped. You cannot sow the seed of an apple tree and expect a pear tree to grow. What you sow is what you get, but if you for a little moment, sow a seed of another kind – a seed of inquisitiveness, a seed of wanting to know spiritual truth, of wanting to develop certain gifts of a psychic and spiritual nature, then you will also reap a harvest, because whatever you give and ask for, you get.

Whether you think of it as negative or positive, you can determine that. It doesn't require great willpower, that's the illusion. People say to me 'yes but I'm hooked on this, but I want to get off it, I want to stop smoking, I want to stop drinking, I want to stop taking drugs, I want to stop doing this……but I can't because I haven't got the willpower'. But I say to them 'you don't need willpower, you just need to make the decision'. You will find that if you do that, very quickly, if you focus your energies on the higher thing that you wish to achieve, it will come flooding into your being and the lower desires will dissipate. It is when you *try* to do something…..and you know this Sunflower, that when you *try* to do something, it implies failure. But when you decide to *be* and you *become*, that is when success is yours."

Amanda spent a few moments talking to Paul here, suggesting that he could use his knowledge to help other youngsters in schools who might be considering taking drugs before the youngster replied, his emotions rising to the surface:

Paul: "If I could turn the clock back I would. Looking ahead, in twenty years time or however long it's going to be, when I've got my own kids I'll know exactly what to watch out for. If they take any kind of pill I will know about it. I'd love to talk to other kids and tell them of the dangers."

White Feather: "To me this is quite clear cut; you either abstain and open up and develop your spiritual gifts or you continue along your current pathway and you leave the higher things until another time. This is why I say that you are at a crossroads because you have come into this knowledge and awareness, which others go through their whole lives without realising. You can ask many, many people much older in years than you, of life after death and they have no understanding or comprehension whatsoever. They have learned very little in their seventy, eighty or ninety years.
So you have come into an awareness and the opportunity is there but you cannot serve two masters – no-one can. You cannot serve two masters! If you try to sit upon two stools what happens? You fall in between them. So you have to decide which master you wish to serve – the master of drugs or the master that is the higher self and the Great Spirit. I know which is the greater force, the greater power and which is the greater drug but it is for you to decide. What I can say to

you is this son; that if you decide to seek the higher, for every effort you make it will be met by a greater effort in my world, because no-one asks and is unheard. Every request for help or guidance is met by a response in my world because your thoughts are known. It was not by mistake that you had the conversation that you had earlier with your mother about certain things. It is not by mistake that I have commented upon those same things even though you say I have no pre-conceived knowledge of them. So all things are for a purpose."

Paul: "How would I make a request? You say that I will be heard, but how will I know? If I wanted to change and do what you suggest, how would I know?"

White Feather: "Well let me put it to you this way; let us suppose that you make a decision and your intent then, is to begin spiritual development, what I would advise you to do after a little while - I am not going to say that it will all be handed to you on a plate because you have to earn it, is to test us out. Say to us......and it does not matter if you think 'I am talking to myself here'....you do not have to know who your guide or helper is at this point....but say to us, say to that guide or helper whose identity you have yet to determine, 'prove it to me, give me a sign, show me something, give me an answer.' Put a question to them and ask them for an answer. There's an old saying you know, 'test the spirits!' Test us and look for an answer and you will find that it will come to you. It may not be in a blinding flash of light – you know there was another Paul in biblical terms, who had a blinding flash of light on the road to Damascus, but you are your own Paul and you may not have a blinding flash of revelation but you may suddenly have a moments inspiration or thought enter your head or see some event that answers your question. Then you will know."

Paul: *"So will I see that there and then?"*

White Feather: "No, not necessarily."

Paul: *"Will it be the next day or in a few days?"*

White Feather: "Not necessarily. It may be a month away, or six weeks but I can say to you without fear of doubt that if you ask, if you earnestly seek it will be shown to you.
Let me tell you something else son; a part of you has already asked the question! That is why you are here tonight. A part of you, a higher part of you, has already asked that you should have some help with your difficulties and that you should have an opportunity to be shown a way out. You are not aware of that consciously but events have conspired and transpired to open doorways, to make relationships, to bring about certain events that have lead to you being here tonight. That is as a result of a higher part of yourself asking that and this is the answer to it.
What I am saying to you now is that you can begin to ask consciously. You can say, in your moments of quietness and stillness 'I want an answer to this question. I want to know something, please give me an answer.'
It will come to you. Not there and then, but it will come to you. That's what you must do."

Paul: *"Hmmm."*

White Feather: "Does that help you?"

Paul: "Yes."

White Feather: "Am I good?" [Laughter]

It had been a quite remarkable evening and it was evident to all that the guide had reached into Paul's heart and made a deep impression upon him. Sensing that the sitting had run its course and that a valuable work had been accomplished, Amanda brought the proceedings to a close, allowing White Feather himself, the final word and a hint at something more:

Amanda: "May I thank you for taking the time to speak to us all tonight and for the help and inspiration that you have given to us. It is our privilege to be with you. We will take your words and love with us in our hearts. Please accept our gratitude and thanks."

White Feather: "And you also, mine. May I thank you all for the privilege of being able to enter into your energies and I find a certain familiarity and a comfort there. I hope that what I have given to you will go far beyond the boundaries of this room. I am glad that the spoken word, the questions, the conversation and everything else has been recorded faithfully by your machine. You may wonder what other things are added to your tape, but I hope that you may play it on more than one occasion and that the words and the intent carried within it may carry far and that like a stone dropped into the lake, the ripples may radiate and touch many. God bless you all and thank you for the opportunity once more."

"It is never the totality of self that comes into form"

Three

Knowing the soul

The term 'soul' is one that is often used to describe the higher aspect of a living form that survives death. Some people believe that only humans have a soul, whilst others state that animals and other life forms also possess this quality. Speaking through his medium before an audience that had come to witness his philosophy, the guide, having opened with his usual greeting, began his address by referring to a question that he was often asked:

White Feather:"You know, many times on these occasions I am asked questions and questions are the life-blood of these evenings. It is through questioning that answers can be forthcoming, although within each answer there is another question. But it is through this that progress can be made and each of you can take a step forward along your infinite pathway of unfoldment. One of the questions that I am often asked is 'What is the soul'? You know, you often hear it spoken about, you often hear the term mentioned frequently in the circles in

Knowing the soul

which you move, when you say 'my soul told me to do this' or 'I am reaching out to my higher self, my soul'. But what is the soul? Do you know what the soul is? There are many interpretations of it, but to me the soul is the Great Spirit within, which in mankind is individualised. You see, you are all parts of God, you are all parts of the Great Spirit. You are never separate from the Great Spirit but the soul in human form, *is the Great Spirit* that has attained individual expression.

Let me explain what I mean; you as part of the Great Spirit have always been, you have always existed. Now, that in a sense is difficult to comprehend because in your three dimensional, material universe, you are familiar only with beginnings, middle bits and endings! Everything seems to be finite. It seems to come into birth, live its life and then perish. But that is only a small part of the picture because the Great Spirit has no beginning and no ending. If you think of the Great Spirit for simplicity's sake, as being a circle or a globe, then where is the beginning or the end? You have always been a part of that but you have not always had the same soul expression and individual status that you now have. You have to realise that the spirit of which you are a part comes through all form. Whether animate or inanimate, complex or simple, mighty or minute, it comes through it. It expresses through the tiniest particle, the tiniest sub-atomic frequency. It expresses through the most distant galaxy in the farthest part of the universe. It comes through the highest evolved soul and the lowest of the low, but its expression is in accordance with the form through which it comes. It has come in your case, through every form that is. You have come through the atom, through the insect, through the plant, through the bird, through the fish, through the ape. Not *you the individual* that you think you are, but *you as part of the Great Spirit*. When that energy, that mind, that intelligence comes into human form such as yours, it attains an individual status and that individuality is never lost. You don't go backwards. You don't come back in another life, into an animal form, or a tree or a plant or an insect. You have done that. You've been there, the spirit within you has come through that. When you reach the point of human form then your soul quality is quickened. Your soul has an individual status."

White Feather went on to explain that it was never the totality of the soul that reincarnated at any one time but only a facet of it:

"Now that said, it is never the totality of the self that comes into form. When you look in the mirror and you see yourself and you think 'that's me, that's who I am. I have a name, I have a form, I have an identity' - that is not the totality of you. It is only a facet. If you think of the soul as being like a diamond, with many such facets, it is only one facet that comes into expression in the physical body at any time. That facet cannot contain the whole. The lesser cannot contain the greater and you as an individual cannot contain the whole that is your soul - just as your soul cannot contain the whole that is the Great Spirit. And yet, it is a part of that. It is rather like trying to put the whole of the ocean of your planet earth into an egg cup. It is an impossibility and yet the cup can contain the essence of all that is in the ocean. This is what you must understand. You are never separate. In that sense you have infinite capacity, infinite ability. You have infinite progress to make because all things are achievable. The highest of the high in my world is linked to the lowest of the low. Where you are, is somewhere in-between, but you have within you the capacity for greatness and infinite expression. It is all a matter of how you can achieve it and this is where the big question comes in."

Revealing his sense of humour - a quality often portrayed by spirit guides, the sage focused on a common human trait as he continued with his talk:

"What is the big question? How often have you all said to yourselves…..now be honest…I'm not coming back here again? *[audience laughter]*. I don't want to come back here again! I've heard you say it and you know, *you* determine whether you come back here again. The Great Spirit doesn't make you come back. No one stands over you with a great stick. What determines whether you come back is how you have lived your life and what degree of the soul's expression you have been able to manifest. The higher that you can become, in terms of spiritual progress, the more of the divinity of the higher aspect of your being you can exhibit and express, the less likelihood it is that you will create Karma – the less likelihood it is that you need to come back. But you know the great stumbling block? It is the ego. What is the ego? The ego is not all that you think it is. You think that the ego is that part of you that has a big head don't you? The part that thinks it is 'the great I am' The part that wants the limelight, the part that thinks it is wonderful. Well, that is only part of it. The ego is a kind of counter-balance if you like, to the soul. But the ego is full of it's own self-importance and seeks always to protect itself and enrich itself for what it is. It thinks that it is the 'I'. It thinks that it is the most important thing. It is not. You have to overcome the ego because the ego in you, creates Karma. The ego in you creates error. The ego in you brings about circumstances in which you stumble and

Knowing the soul

fall, in which you make mistakes. Now this is all very well to a point, because you learn from these things, but when the ego becomes more important than the soul, then you are in trouble, you are in difficulty. And if you look around you in your world you will see that the cause of all conflicts, all distress and illness and disease and suffering and all that holds back the soul, has its roots in ego.

Now you may say 'well hang on a minute.....how can this be? What about someone who is born into your world, who has not asked to come and who is born perhaps with a great deformity, where is the ego there?' But you have to look back. You have to look at the bigger picture. You have to realise what that soul has done in previous lifetimes. What has been its pathway? What has been its journey? What circumstances has it created that has brought it back again into substance, into matter, to experience these situations? Because make no mistake my friends, Karma has to be outworked, it has to be overcome, it has to be beaten in that sense and where do you correct the imbalance? You can't do it in my world. You have to do it in your world where it was created. It's no good sweeping it under the carpet or thinking that when death occurs and you pass into my world, all that lifetime's experiences and events are gone forever. They are not. You have created that, so you have to fix it. You have to put it right. You have to outwork it and if you find this occurring time and time again, that you are coming to the same crossroads, then you have to look and question yourself and you have to say 'is this the soul that is doing this or is it the ego?" You will find more often than not that the ego has created the imbalance and the soul has to try and put it right. But when you think then of what the soul is, do not think of the soul as being something outside of you. Don't think of it as some do as being like some balloon on the end of a string that you can tug now and again when you want to gain access to it. The soul is neither within nor without and yet is both. Think of yourself as a facet of your soul. Recognise that you are here to outwork certain aspects of your pathway, to pay off Karmic debt and to render a service to your fellow man and so quicken your own vibrations. And if you can go beyond that 'little self' that you think is so important - the great I AM, if you can put aside ego, put aside self, put aside all that you would do to feed yourself in that sense, at the exclusion of others, if you can become egoless not egotistical, if you can become selfless not selfish and if you can become altruistic, if you can serve, then you will find that you will make progress more quickly than you could ever imagine. This truly will be coming into fulfilment of your soul's purpose. Something to think about!"

The spirit communicator had indeed given those present something to think about, as he so often does. Following an address such as this, questions inevitably abound and here the guide truly comes into his own as he replies to those looking for more answers:

Question: "Can you clarify what is meant by the terms 'soul mates', 'group soul' and 'twin souls' and do soul mates keep the same gender?"

White Feather: "I think it is important for me to clarify what is meant by these expressions as the problem of semantics can confuse the issue. I can speak only of that which I know and if others wish to use a different terminology that is their prerogative. Let me state clearly that there are what I call group souls or soul groups which comprise a collection of individual, like-minded souls that exist and operate together at relatively the same level of spiritual awareness and development. These groups are not necessarily highly developed but nevertheless retain a common consciousness. Individuals within these groups are what I refer to as affinities.

Soul mates however, are aspects of one individualised soul, facets if you like of the one whole, which may on rare occasions incarnate at the same time through different earthly bodies. The term 'twin souls' is I suspect, what some people refer to when they are speaking about their concept of soul mates.

Regarding whether or not soul mates keep the same gender for successive incarnations, this is not set in stone, for the spirit in essence is neither male nor female and yet expresses through both forms whilst incarnate. I have to say however, in my experience it is commonplace that if two facets of the one diamond incarnate at the same time, they usually, although not exclusively, take opposing male and female forms."

Question: "If one member of a group soul reincarnates upon the earth is it possible for them to remember a previous incarnation of another member of that soul group?"

White Feather: "It is possible, but unlikely. Group souls by their very definition are composed of a collective of like-minded, spiritually harmonious individuals and naturally where there have been and continue to be, strong connections and past lives have been shared, then there could be some memory traces which are recountable under the right circumstances during another reincarnation, due to the fact that they could exert a detrimental influence on the current incarnation. I would advise caution, scrutiny and the use of common sense when analysing any information given or retrieved that purports to be from the past life of another, as it can be open to distortion due to the mechanics involved."

It seems that not only are we as individuals, part of larger group souls but also the animal kingdom. In an earlier communication featured in 'Answers for an Enquiring Mind' White Feather referred to our so called 'lesser brethren' as being part of a wider group consciousness but also emphasised the fact that it is only when the same spirit that operates through them reaches the level of humanity that it attains individual expression:

"Now the animals to which we are referring for the purposes of this talk tonight are part of a group soul, part of a group consciousness and through the suffering that is being undertaken by them upon the earth, that group consciousness is progressing. It is being compensated and ultimately there will be those aspects that, having come through that level of being will come into a higher form of being such as the human and when that is reached, there the soul has individual status."

He also went on to explain that the consciousness that operates at the animal level, having experienced and progressed to attain a higher expression, does not regress back to that level:

"You, having come through those lower forms, will never return to that level. Even though you may come back time and time again upon the earth through different human forms you will not go back into that group consciousness because you have attained an individual status and it is for you to continue on your upward journey through your world and through mine, ever progressing."

Whether human or animal, it seems clear that the same intelligence operates through all levels of creation. From what White Feather and other notable teachers tell us, that creative force expresses itself in ever greater degree as it moves into and through more evolved forms. In the case of this earth, when it reaches expression through mankind it appears to attain an individual status whilst still remaining part of a larger collective of like minds. This makes perfect sense, because even though our beloved animals, like our human counterparts, return to us after death to prove their continued existence, it does not necessarily follow that they have an individualised soul. They are it would seem, still part of the group soul of their species and although contact with humanity allows them to retain certain aspects of their personality relating to specific incarnations, it is not retained at that level for all time.

The human soul appears to retain that quality and even though successive incarnations create vastly different personalities undergoing a wide range of experiences, the overall essence and unique evolution of each soul is maintained for eternity.

We can but speculate as to the future of our soul's evolution. White Feather has stated many times that even though we are parts of larger entities, we never lose our individuality.

We shall surely discover the answers to the mystery of the soul as our pathway unfolds, but one thing above all else seems beyond doubt; we are infinite souls upon an eternal journey to light and understanding.

"If you can touch the soul then you are indeed doing the work of the Great Spirit"

Four
Amongst Healers

One dark winter evening in early 2007 we invited a friend and local therapist along for a sitting with White Feather. Donna came with an open mind and warm heart for her meeting with the spirit master and left, having been touched deeply by the quality of his communication. Amanda, who is also a Reiki Master and Teacher added her own vital contribution to the proceedings and was welcomed warmly by the guide as he made his entrance:

"May I embrace you all with the divine love of the Great Spirit. Sunflower! I'm just checking that you are there!"

Amanda: "I am. It's really nice to talk to you."

White Feather: "It's been a little while but it is always a privilege that our streams of energy can again unite together in the greater ocean of consciousness, that through this we may bathe in the waters of truth and understanding. For it is truth, as I have said so frequently and with so much passion, that is the liberator of souls. In your world, truth is at a premium, which is why we always celebrate whenever the barriers can be surmounted and the divine light can begin to shine into the dark crevices of your earthly domain. Because where there is light, darkness is vanquished. Where there is truth, ignorance dissipates. Where there is love, there, anger and hostility have nowhere to run.

I want to thank you for enabling me to be here with you tonight and I am fully aware of the purpose of this meeting and I am in absolute concord with what we have to undertake and the reasons behind it. This is why I want to begin if I may, by saying a few words to you on the subject of healing because I know through joining through this instrument with your energies that you both embrace the healing faculty which you have not only developed within your being but for which you each also have natural qualities that you bring to your work. This of course, is a prerequisite of any healer. There are those who like to think of themselves as healers but their work is limited for they have not the necessary constitution to apply to their work. But where you have empathy or you have compassion, or you have qualities that have been developed over many lifetimes, there is an added dimension to your work and you can be truly employed by the energies of the spirit that seek to bring their rich beneficence to those who are in need of it.

When you give your healing, whatever discipline it is that you work through, whatever aspect you employ, whatever angle you take, what is it that you are healing? If you are attempting to relieve suffering of the physical body by removing discomfort, by alleviating pain, bringing hope where there is despair, bringing joy where there is sorrow, mending damaged limbs, trying to repair minds that are in turmoil, then you are doing a great work. Whether you employ the use of oils, whether you use 'hands on' and link with other minds who can use you as an instrument or whether you are a surgeon who uses a scalpel, you are operating in a way that is to be commended for any who seek to alleviate the difficulties of others are doing a great work. So if you can heal at the physical level that is one thing, but if you can heal not only the *effect*, that is to say the illness or discomfort itself, but the *cause* of the effect, then you are working at an even deeper level, because it is one thing to take away pain and suffering in that sense, but it another to address the cause of that suffering. If you can touch the cause of the suffering and thus prevent a re-occurrence of the malady, whatever it might be, then you have undertaken indeed, a great work.

But, there is another level at which you can work, because if you can touch the soul then you are indeed doing the work of the Great Spirit. What do we mean by 'touching the soul?' Well, every illness and disease is an effect of a cause. That cause may originate upon any number of levels from any manner of means, but behind the cause of that effect is an even deeper cause. You may think that by removing the immediate cause and by addressing the initial cause of the illness, you are healing and in a sense you are, but there may be a greater cause, a deeper cause beyond that initial one. Do you see what I am saying? That may be far deeper than you at first realise. It may go back to past lives. It may have a far deeper origination. That is why, if you can blend with your work, the truly spiritual powers that bring with them the deepest and most profound energies, then you can awaken the soul and touch the soul. When you touch the soul with your healing then a truly wonderful transformation can take place that sees a revitalisation, realignment, a total alteration in the state of mind, spirit and body that will ultimately prevent disharmony from occurring again.

Let me give you an example; let us suppose that one has a particular malady that won't respond to any medical treatment of the orthodox type, one can, through healing, bring about a change in that discomfort, that alleviates pain but also allows the individual to realise that perhaps their thoughts, their actions, their emotions have had some contribution in bringing about the particular malady that has afflicted them. So you are working there, on a physical and also a mental and emotional level and touching upon the spiritual. But if you can look deeper, if you can through your spiritual abilities go even beyond that and realise that at some deeper level there has been trauma or imbalance that has occurred and if you can make that individual aware of the great divine power that they have within themselves, to transform and bring about healing from within, then you are truly, truly making a profound impact upon them. Because make no mistake, where there is true awareness and ignorance is banished then there can be no illness, there can be no discomfort, because mind, body and spirit are aligned as one. What is illness? What is discomfort? What is pain? It is the body's way of responding to a situation and normally it is the result of a law being activated because another law has been transgressed. If through wrong actions, wrong thoughts, wrong application an imbalance has occurred, then illness is the result and pain and suffering follow. Very often, those conditions originate not in the physical world, but on the mental plane or even the emotional or the spiritual planes because where imbalances are brought about, brought into being, there are blockages and there is all manner of vibrational conflicts. It is rather like gears that have been put against each other so that their synchronicity is lost, they are out of mesh with each other and so they come to a standstill. Where there is friction, this results, ultimately in disease affecting the physical form.

So when you are working as you do in your healing centre or whatever approach you take, always try to embrace the holistic. Look at the total self of the individual whom you are treating. Realise that they are physical, mental, emotional, spiritual beings and that to work upon one level, one layer, as admirable as it is, very often does not provide a total solution. If you treat the individual as a total being, a multi-dimensional, many faceted individual, then you have more chance of success and where an initial approach is made through one particular discipline in your world, that can flow into others. Realise that the only limits that you have upon your work are those which you allow, which you place upon yourself. You are an instrument of the spirit, never forget that and the more that you can be open and receptive to the power that seeks to work through you, the greater will be your impact and the more wondrous and fulfilling the results."

White Feather had as always, raised some interesting points and it was clear that he had tried to offer a deeper insight into the causes of illness and the need to adopt a more holistic approach when offering treatment. It seemed that his words had already made an impact:

Donna: "Thank you White Feather. It is a tremendous privilege to be here and to be able to watch and learn. I hope you'll forgive me if some of my questions are naive but I just want to try and get more understanding so that I can take this forward into anything that I am *able to do.*

As an individual in this world, is there one spirit or more than one spirit drawn to or likely to be working with me?"

White Feather: "Everyone who seeks earnestly to work in ways that alleviate suffering and open themselves up to the almighty power of the spirit, draws to themselves a band of helpers which are often many in number. There can be several who seek to work with you because where one will find that their particular qualities and strengths can be utilised in one way of another, another within the group may have more success, or less success depending upon how they can link through you. Just as in your world you have doctors, surgeons, nurses and so on, who each bring their own qualities, their own skills to bear in treating a particular individual or group of people, so it is with my world. No-one has a monopoly upon wisdom and understanding and it is sometimes more beneficial that one should step forward to work through you and then allow another, if they are able to link in sufficient strength, to utilise your capabilities and to work also in their way.

So we try different things. Sometimes we find that one individual is more easily able to link through you and so takes upon themselves the role of the head helper in my world, who opens the links with you, opens the doors, and others then join on that same vibration to work through you. It is a very ordered way in which we work and sometimes would be a little more complex than we would have you believe! But ultimately there are many within the group who work with you. You are never left alone and we always try to bring to bear the greatest power that we can through you as an instrument to work upon the patient and alleviate suffering where we can."

Donna: "Is there anyway I can open myself up to be more aware of a single spirit?"

White Feather: "Well, that of course is always possible but you know that I always say to people that it's not as important that you know who works *with* you, but what is put *through* you - the message that is brought through, the healing that is brought through, the work that is achieved, the work that is undertaken. I always in my own case emphasise that it is the message rather than the messenger that is of the greatest import. However, if it is necessary and if it is beneficial for all parties that you should become aware of those who work with you from my side of life, then we will have no hesitation in stepping forward when you are able to receive our messages and to let you know that. But initially I would say to you; concentrate on your attunement, on your linking with the spirit world and those who are drawn to you because attunement is the key to the power that seeks to operate through you. If you can attune to it then you will find that all else will follow, all else will fall into place."

Donna: "Can you explain a little bit more about attunement and how I can attune myself in that way?"

White Feather: "Sunflower, you are a musician aren't you? You know about attunement. You know that if you strike a note through a tuning fork that has a particular pitch, it will resonate or vibrate. You will find that through this vibrational energy other objects in the near vicinity will resonate in sympathy with it. If you are undertaking the task of tuning an instrument then you will find that you can adjust the keys or the strings, or the notes to the same pitch as the tuning fork so that there is perfect resonance between the one and the other and that, in simple terms is what attunement means. If you can raise your mind above the lower material thoughts that occupy your days, if you can put aside concerns of a material nature and the mundane tasks which you have to undertake and allow your spirit to soar like an eagle way above the trees, then you will find that you will appear to us as a light and we will be drawn to you on the same vibratory desire to serve and there will be a resonance between us. We will more easily be able to access your energies, your mind, your unconscious capability, that through this we can put whatever we are able through you. Always remember that what comes, comes *through* you. It is not *from* you, it comes through you."

Recognising that healing takes many forms and is not owned by any individual or group, Amanda asked the sage whether there was any significant difference in approach between one discipline and another:

Amanda: "Can I just ask White Feather……as Reiki healers, we are taught to attune to a life force energy, that's what 'Reiki' means, so when we are talking about linking with spiritual healers in the spirit world how does that come into it? Are we linking first with a person in spirit [a spirit guide] or are we first of all linking with that life force energy and within that life force energy there are specific individual healers who might be drawn to our healing energy?"

White Feather: "Yes, I am aware of Reiki and I know of the work that is undertaken which is very, very good work. Labels of course are of little interest to me but in essence you are linking with something that is beyond your normal consciousness, beyond your physical vibration. Whether you term that 'life energy' or 'spiritual energy', 'Chi'.....whatever you want to call it – it is the energy of life and if you can attune first in the way that you have been taught, in the way that you find familiar and with which you find an ease and a comfort, that is the way that you should proceed. Always remember that for any healing endeavour, when one in your world attunes, there is always one in my world who works with them because you are never alone. Whether you believe or accept that you are attuning to a spirit or to a life force energy doesn't matter. What matters is that you are attuning to an energy that is greater than you are and you are offering yourselves as channels.

Now think about this; if you think of a simple reed - you have played an instrument haven't you?.....you know that within the wind instrument there is a reed – you have the two aspects of the reed that make the sound. One could simplify this further and speak of two blades of grass – perhaps as a child you did this when you held two blades of grass between your fingers and blew through them and produced a kind of a raspberry sound! Well, the fact is, that here is a divine principle at work because here you have two aspects at work, uniting together in silence to enable the breath of the spirit to produce the sound through them. What happens with any form of healing that is non-physical is that you have two aspects coming together – you the healer and the energy, whether you call it life force energy or whether you call it attunement to spiritual energy, coming together and here it is that the power can function through a combination of the two aspects. That is what matters."

Amanda: "What importance then, do you put on the healer being disciplined in their own protection and in the way that they attune? Does that affect the quality of the healing?"

White Feather: "Well everything that the healer from your world…..the instrument, does, affects the quality of the power that comes through him, everything. The well being, the mental state, the emotional state, the spiritual progress or lack of it, all of these are contributory factors to the way in which spirit energy can operate through an instrument.
As for protection, I sometimes have a little smile to myself when I see some in your world undertaking elaborate procedures to ensure that they are protected. What you have to realise is that the protection that you evoke is self-generated by your intent, by your application, by your spiritual progress, by your desire and the character that you are and where you sit earnestly in love, with the right intent, you naturally bring about a protection around you because you carry and express the divine light and the light is always stronger than the darkness of ignorance.
Where you have problems arising it is through ignorance, through superstition and through tampering and meddling with things that people know very little about. In the normal sense where you have a balanced individual whose desire is to serve, the protection is automatic. Does that answer your question?"

Amanda: "Yes thank you."

As the sitting progressed, the topic of 'protection' came up again and the spirit guide was quick to point out that he had little time for some of the more intricate techniques that seem to be employed by some when opening up to the spirit world:

Donna: *"I find that very comforting White Feather, because we are introduced to all sorts of elaborate ideas to protect ourselves. I've been introduced to using crystals as a form of protection, what do you think about that?"*

White Feather: "Well if you find that it helps, then by all means follow it but it is not necessary, that's what I am saying. It is not necessary. It is another link in the chain that if it helps you, if it comforts you, if it assists you in your work then by all means pursue it but what better protection is there than your own mental state, your thoughts and your intent? If you always direct those things to the highest, if your motive is always selfless, if it is filled with altruism, with kindness, with love, with the higher spiritual motives, that is the protection that you need, nothing else. These props that people have, that they think carry so much power.....they don't really. The greatest power is always within. If you look back through the centuries of time, you will see that some of the greatest healers ever to walk upon your world had no props, no crystals, no 'openings of chakras' no reciting of mantras, no standing in circles or any of this. They simply opened themselves to the power of the divine spirit and the power of the spirit poured through them like a great gushing fountain. This is true healing."

Amanda: *"The only concern I've got is that out of the healing sanctuary as it were, in normal walks of life we sometimes come into contact with people whom we perhaps wouldn't choose to be with. When we sense the energies are not particularly helpful and vibrations not as positive as our own, is there some measure of natural protection? Also, if we as humans are perhaps not in the right frame of mind and the thoughts we are giving out are not as valid as they might be, where do we stand then?"*

White Feather: "Well, that is your Achilles heal in a sense because if you allow yourself to be distracted and in some way lower your guard shall we say and almost enter into a facet of their energies then you are in some degree leaving yourself vulnerable. You do have a spiritual protection that I've already outlined to you, that you develop and the more that you work with the power of the spirit the stronger your protection is and you can, if you wish to visualise that, think of it as a kind of protective bubble. It is in fact part of your own aura that you take with you wherever you go. But you know yourself, however much protection you have, if you are standing in front of a train it will run you over. If you jump off a bridge you will invariably give up your physical body and pass into my world! These things have an impact, because it is matter against matter, physical form against physical form and all the protection in my world and all the protection in your world won't save you from that. That is a consequence of natural law. So you have to use a measure of common sense, clear-headedness, clear thinking and realise that sometimes you have to take other measures. You have to sometimes withdraw, sometimes get reinforcements – the help of others, as well as install certain procedures and disciplines that should be followed. So it is I think, wise to use a combination of measures and not to rely merely upon your own self protection, however strong that might be. Do you think that is wise?"

Amanda: "Yes that's very helpful, thank you."

Donna: "You touched upon our mortality earlier, have we all been here before and if so, how does spirit evolve? How does spirit come about, to be in the human form? And is there a hierarchy in spirit?"

White Feather: "How many questions is that?"

Donna [laughing]: "I'm so sorry....it's just my enthusiasm to hear what you've got to say!"

White Feather: "You know me well Sunflower don't you?"

Amanda: "I do know you well, yes."

White Feather: "I don't know which one to take first. First of all, there is the Great Spirit or God — whatever label you wish to call it, the divine intelligence behind all of life. The Great Spirit always was, always is and always shall be. It has no beginning and no end. You are a part of that, therefore you have had no beginning and will know no finality. In that sense the Great Spirit has nothing to learn, because the Great Spirit knows everything. The Great Spirit is all wise and all knowing and all of that wisdom, all of that knowledge will always be there. It has always been there. But because you are like a seed sent forth into the garden of life, you have yet to recognise that same divinity within you. You are imperfect, or your expression is imperfect. The expression of the divine through you is imperfect because you as an individualised facet of the whole are imperfect. You have to unfold that imperfection through many, many lifetimes, through many visits to this world and perhaps to many other worlds in many forms, male and female, to undergo all of life's vast panorama, life's vast spectrum of conditions; good and bad, light and dark, negative and positive, high and low, complex and simple, mighty and minute, that through this you come into a realisation of the divine within you. That slowly, imperceptibly, over many, many lives you will hone your innate abilities. They come to the surface and your spirit quickens. You become enriched, you become aware. You realise that all of these worlds upon which you pass through many lifetimes are illusionary. You come to realise that the true essence is that which lies within, which is of the divine spirit. That is why you come here.

So in the purest sense, the Great Spirit is already perfect, but its expression through the likes of you and I and countless other billions of life forms is imperfect. It is we who are learning, not the Great Spirit. It is we as facets of the whole who are learning to express the latent divinity within us and so re-unite in a sense and become one with the perfect wisdom that already resides somewhere deep within us."

With Donna gaining in confidence from the fluent replies that were emanating from the spirit control, she ventured to ask a question concerning the darker side of the spirit planes which in turn drew a lengthy reply from the teacher:

Donna: "We talk about spirits, particularly when we are doing Reiki, only doing good. What about evil acts and how can we protect ourselves?"

White Feather: "Well again, there is evil in your world, there is evil in my world — don't think that everything in the spirit world is sunshine and light because it isn't. In the higher realms which I am fortunate enough to inhabit, there is harmony, there is light, there is wisdom. But at the lower levels of my world there is ignorance, there is darkness, there is evil. Evil is not something separate from the Great Spirit —the Great Spirit is within all things, but evil comes about as a result of the ignorance of the mind. The ignorance in mans' case is of the mind, brought about by his lower ego states, by his lower emotional states and by his thinking. Where he adheres to selfishness, to greed, to all of the lower emotions, through this emerges evil within his thoughts and his actions. You will find evil exists in many, many places but it doesn't mean that you will have to embrace it because if you always attune yourself to the higher, to the light, then you will find that evil cannot really touch you. I am not saying that you will have a life free of difficulty or that you will have a life free of pain or suffering, because these things are sometimes brought about as a way of allowing your soul to learn and quicken, but embracing evil is quite something else and you will find that where there is a degree of spiritual awareness and knowledge, it is easy to turn away from evil. Because evil is something that comes from the lower states of mind, from the lower ego states of man's mind and where there is a recognition that no good can come from it, then it is that you are given the strength sufficient to resist it.

So I would say to you again, referring to my earlier discussion about protection, that protection comes to you automatically when you grow spiritually. When you grow spiritually then your thoughts change, your vision changes, your whole vibrations change and you actually create around you a spiritual strength within your aura, your energy fields and this brings you a protection against lower forces.

One thing I would say is that always you have free will, you can choose. There are some who decide to choose the pathway of evil. That is their choice - we cannot interfere with what man chooses to do. If man chooses evil then that is mans' responsibility. All that I am saying to you is that where there is knowledge, where there is wisdom, where there is understanding, where there is spiritual growth, it is highly unlikely that such an individual would choose a pathway of evil. It is contrary to the very laws of life that operate, because where there is spiritual wisdom, there the individual inevitably chooses the pathway of light and progress because he has already recognised the wondrous power that resides within."

Having found the answer a satisfactory one, Donna then switched her questioning to that of children - with an enquiry that White Feather took great delight in answering:

Donna: "About children…..are they linked to us spiritually?"

White Feather: "The simple answer to that is yes, because if a child is born of you then the soul aspect that has chosen to link through that child born through you has drawn to you because there is a familiarity, there is a connection, there is an attraction. You have heard of the saying 'like attracts like'? …..at some level there is an attraction between the incarnating spirit and the one through whom it comes and I use the term to include both the male and the female energies that bring about the conception, the vehicle through which one is about to reincarnate. There has to be some link there.
However, to take that a little further, undoubtedly there are deeper, more profound spiritual connections between some than others and you very often find that in past lives, where individuals have lived and experienced all manner of conditions together, it binds them, unites them and where there is love there is no separation. Very often they will choose to reincarnate again together in a future life, where the

roles perhaps are reversed, where the child becomes the mother, where the mother becomes the child. These differences are not of the greatest import, what matters is that as spiritual individuals they have forged a connection. Perhaps they have Karma to outwork, perhaps they choose to reincarnate to help each other or other members of their spiritual family - because recognise this; that you do not incarnate in isolation. If you could see with the eyes of the spirit you would recognise that many members of your family, even though you may not like them this time around for whatever reasons, or even if you feel a great empathy and love towards them, you have lived before on this world and you have perhaps a little unfinished business to do -some Karma to outwork or some service to render!

So the answer to your question is that yes, very often there is a deeper spiritual connection between one and another."

Donna: "Has everyone got a guardian angel watching over them?"

White Feather: "People in your world often use many names to refer to certain aspects and as to helpers in my world, they may be referred to as guardian angels, some think of them as angels, others as simply helpers or guardians…..all manner of labels. What matters is that they are like you, human in every respect, but they are drawn to you because they have an affinity with you. Either because you have lived together before and they wish to help you in this lifetime and render spiritual service, as well as advancing their own spiritual pathway or because you have work to do of a spiritual nature. Perhaps you are a medium, perhaps you are in some way a vessel for the power of the spirit and they will help you in that way. So it doesn't matter what label you want to put upon them, they will be with you.

You each have helpers surrounding you. All who are hearing these words or reading these words, must know that they are never alone. You each have helpers and loved ones who surround you. We try to look out for you, we try to do our best to guide you to a degree and to protect you. But as I said earlier, you have free will and your own choices, your own decisions in life must be taken into account. If you choose to undertake a particular course of action we can only try to advise you differently, but ultimately it is your decision. We cannot prevent you sometimes, from taking a certain course of action. So in that sense, we are a little impotent to an extent, but always where there is a receptive heart and a receptive mind, we will do our best to provide guidance and wisdom."

With Amanda listening intently whilst also giving forth her own energies to assist the guide, she intervened in the proceedings with perhaps one of the most profound questions the sage had ever been asked:

Amanda: *"Could I just ask you a question please? Is it possible that there are parallel lifetimes that are going on at the same time as this one, with different choices being made? I find this a difficult concept to grasp but I am interested in what you have got to say about it."*

White Feather: "You know Sunflower, that I can only deal in facts. Always, whenever I impart my answers, to whatever questions I am asked from whatever source, I deliver my replies based upon the facts that I have at my disposal and the knowledge and wisdom that I have been able to acquire……"

Amanda: "I value that. That's why I am asking you."

White Feather: "……from a factual point of view, although I am aware of this theory, I have no factual evidence to support it. That does not mean to say that it is not true, but I can only speak from the level at which I find myself in my spiritual progress and the knowledge and information to which I have access and my ability to operate through this instrument. Combining all of those things together I have no factual evidence or experience to support the view that you are purporting.
However, one has to think of these things and I have heard of this theory. I have heard of the scientific discussions that have taken place and if you think within it, what your scientists are suggesting is that an individual has many parallel lifetimes that run side by side continuously. That is what you are saying isn't it?"

Amanda: "Well that's what I've been considering because I've been reading a book that has made me think about it."

White Feather: "Yes…..well if that were so, then one would assume that there would be an infinite number of lifetimes, an infinite number of parallel experiences, and infinite number of universes…..there would have to be, because there are an infinite number of combinations of experiences that *could* happen. Do you see what I am saying? In that sense, it would almost make redundant the life journey from ignorance to truth because it wouldn't matter whatever one learned in this lifetime, there would always be this continual sequence of parallel lifetimes occurring with an almost innumerable combination of events, do you see what I am saying?"

Amanda: "Hmmm…..and innumerable choices which to make any sense of going from ignorance to truth means that at some point we do have to make a decision and follow that through."

White Feather: "Absolutely. So one has to ask oneself, where would this end? Now of course the Great Spirit is infinite, life is infinite and you have heard me say that you never reach perfection, but I cannot quite come to the acceptance, with where I am at the moment in my own progression, that there are an infinite number of parallel universes with an infinite number of continuous experiences running in tandem with each other. I can only deal with what I know now, with the individual that I am, with the pathways that I have walked and which I have knowledge of, through past lives. In that sense there are many, many lives but in the sense of which you are speaking I have no factual evidence to back it up and I find difficulty with the acceptance of it. That's my truthful answer."

Relishing the conversation that was now unfolding, Amanda followed up her original question with an equally intriguing one that had its roots in her understanding of Reiki principles:

Amanda: "Just to follow on from that, if we accept that past, present and future co-exist, is it not possible for our consciousness to visit parts of our past and our future and mould the choices that we might make dependent upon the view of that situation at that time?"

White Feather: "To an extent yes, but it depends upon the level of awareness that one has reached. You cannot state at any one time that you are able to become aware of the totality of past, present and future until you have reached a very high degree of spiritual unfoldment and there are reasons for that of course. The natural sequence of events ensures that every individual progresses in a linear manner through the passage of time and space. Now, time in my world is different from time in your world because we are somewhat elevated in terms of our spiritual awareness and also the frequency of vibration of our whole being is different. So we are not subject to the same grossness, the same heaviness that matter obtains, but nevertheless there is a sequence, a movement, a direction if you like.

You may have heard of the 'arrow of time'. The arrow of time is suggestive of a movement from past to future and quite clearly if that arrow of time did not exist and at the level of progression that we find ourselves we were able to reverse it, to have the past following the present or the future, or even to become fully aware of past, present and future then there are certain things that we would not learn. There are certain lessons that we would not undergo and our very spiritual progress and indeed our whole nature would be threatened. Do you see that?

One has to follow this process of cause and effect. Of learning, making mistakes, of falling down and getting up, of progress. This is what progress is and it is only when one reaches the very highest levels of spiritual awareness that this whole concept of past, present and future becomes more of a substantial reality. Do you understand that?

You are asking very deep questions and I pay tribute to you for that, but you have to realise that the answers, by their very nature can be somewhat complex."

Ensuring that she had fully understood the implications within

White Feathers' complex reply, Amanda pressed the guide for further clarification:

Amanda: "Just to explain further from a healing perspective, if you say the arrow of time goes forward, are we able to send that arrow back in time with distant healing, to heal past traumas?"

White Feather: "I have my doubts on that I have to say, because you are then imposing upon the nature of cause and effect."

Amanda: "Yes, that's what has brought up my question."

White Feather: "How can you interfere with what has had a cause and an effect? You have to see that even though the idea is a nice one - one could almost say a romantic one and certainly some who undertake it like to think that they have some kind of power, that they can do this and send healing back to the past, it's not quite as simple as that. Cause and effect are inalterable in their operation, in their sequence. They are part of a chain – cause, effect, effect, cause, cause, effect.....so it goes on. Do you understand that?"

Amanda: "Yes. So we might be better using the distant healing to help that particular person into an awareness of that cause and effect and to initiate their own healing?"

White Feather: "I think that would be more profitable. Let me just add one thing though to this; you know through your work with the mind that you can travel back through the memory of past events and sometimes through changing the way that an individual *remembers* that past event you can initiate a healing in the *present* moment, do you understand that? That however, doesn't contradict what I have already said because it hasn't affected the sequence of cause and effect that was started many years ago through events that happened and has brought that individual to your doorstep now with whatever ailment or difficulty that they have. You are merely reaching back your hand through the years that have elapsed through time, to open up that doorway into the past, into the 'younger' person and initiating a memory that can be changed, can be manipulated at a mind level. You are not in any way altering in reality, the sequence of cause and effect that has already transpired."

Donna: "So we would try to bring about an acceptance?"

White Feather: "I think that is a good word – acceptance. Or one could say one brings about an awareness in the present moment for that individual, to see something in a way that they hadn't before, to remember something in a different way. People tend to remember things as though they were the only way that they could remember them and they are somehow fixed in solid stone. If you can help them to realise that perhaps they can remember them in a different way, then you are altering their perception and this is what some disciplines, some therapies are able to do in their work - to change the way that the mind perceives the memory of that past. They are not actually changing the past, they are changing the *memory* of the past."

Amanda: "I'm thinking particularly as an example, someone that I work with who is a young woman whose husband died quite suddenly. When she woke up, he was dead beside her. Now she's dealt extremely well with that situation, however the memory of that actual thing happening to her is still something that bothers her a lot. I was wondering how we might help her and is it appropriate to help her to perceive that experience differently now?"

White Feather: "It is only appropriate if that individual deems it appropriate. You cannot interfere with their free will but if they choose to hold that memory and its associated emotions, fear and thoughts in that particular sense, then that is their choice. If however they are spiritually ready and emotionally and mentally open to healing and you can, through your therapeutic knowledge access that trauma and offer them a different perception of it, that is another matter. But it depends upon the individual, you can't force it, as you know."

Picking up on the earlier thread concerning the possibility of sending distant Reiki healing back in time, Donna renewed the questioning by asking if the reverse was possible:

Donna: "You talked about distant Reiki healing, going backwards in time. What are your thoughts on the power of sending Reiki energy forward in time?"

White Feather: "Well again, one has to say there is a little merit in that, but always I come back to the operation of law. It is not quite the same sending it forward as backward, because the law of cause and effect has not yet come into operation. So there is some merit in it, but I must emphasise that the law of cause and effect in its operation, particularly allied to free will, cannot be abrogated. Now you could choose to send healing power to an individual, let us say a member of the family who is going on a particular visit, perhaps to a busy city or travelling abroad, and you send that healing power that they will have a safe journey, they will arrive at their destination and they will be protected, that sort of thing. But their own free will may place them in jeopardy, may put them into circumstances that you would rather they were able to avoid as well as all manner of other aspects that come into the equation. So these things cannot be ignored, they have to be taken into account. That said, I always have stated that an individual is only where they are because they are meant to be there at that time. Their own energies, their own pathway, their own life journey, their own Karma has placed them there. If they are meant to undergo a particular experience, then undergo it they will, because their whole being has put them there. Do you understand?

Now that is not to say that you shouldn't try to send healing, that you shouldn't give healing, that you shouldn't pray for them, that you shouldn't wish them well, because these are admirable human traits that all should strive to imbibe, these are spiritual qualities, but you have to understand that many things, come into the melting pot, many aspects have to be taken into account. You have to look with the eyes of the spirit to gain the whole picture."

Donna: "So is life's journey mapped out for us?"

White Feather: "Only to an extent. There is an overall pattern. There are what I call parameters within which you operate, but I must emphasise that the law of cause and effect and most notably your own freewill can never be discarded. There are certain lessons upon life's pathway that are meant to be learned but whether or not they come to pass is influenced by your actions and by your thoughts. Usually one finds that the major events do come about because the very nature of your being, your constitution and what your soul already knows of you, ensures that you find yourself placed in those circumstances. But always, always your free will has to be taken into account, it can never be discarded and if you choose at any moment to take a completely different pathway then that is your choice, your responsibility. There is little that we can do to change that and that is as it should be. For example; sometimes I am asked the question 'is there a time to die?' and I say well, the soul knows before it comes, the length of time that you are here upon the earth, but if you choose to undertake a lifestyle that threatens that, then you can shorten that life. That is a matter for your own free will and the way that you think and act and behave. If you take substances that are toxic to the body, if you take drugs or other things that harm it then invariably you will shorten its physical span. If you don't then you will outwork the length of time that is allotted to you and that your soul is aware of before you come here upon the earth.

So all of these things come into the equation and the 'bottom line' if I can use your language, is that free will is the guiding principle that underpins this of which I speak."

Donna: "Is our free will shaped by our past life experiences?"

White Feather: "Absolutely. Even though this life that you have is unique – it will never be repeated, there will never be another 'you', because this is a unique experience. However, *you* are an individual and I am speaking now of the difference between the individual 'you' which is eternal and the personality vehicle that you have in this life and that you think of as 'you'. The real you, the individual 'you' has been shaped by its many past lives – the many facets of it that have come into a physical body time and time again in order to learn and gain experience. All of these energies, all of these qualities, all of these strengths and virtues and all of these imperfections and faults are brought together into the mix and it is that, which enables the choice of vehicle in that life to have been made. The vehicle that you have chosen will have certain attributes, certain strengths, certain weaknesses, a certain predisposition to conditions, to illness, to talents, to qualities that you bring out in that life and all of these things are known by the soul. They all contribute to the way that the free will can operate at this level.

You may be born into a genetic vessel that is the result of the combination of the parentage that leaves you with a certain predisposition towards a certain illness, perhaps later in life – let us say a weak heart or a weak spleen or some other physical condition, now your free will has to contend with that. It has to work through it. But the soul, the greater self, will know beforehand that, that is what the facet of it is coming into. It knows that it has to contend with that and it may well even choose it in order that it can learn and so be quickened. Do you see? This is how it evolves."

Amanda: "The instrument through which you speak always says that when he goes back to spirit he doesn't want to come back again! But will he remember that or is that just an element of his personality in this particular lifetime?"

White Feather: "I suspect a little of both. The consciousness will remember it in my world but it is a matter for the higher aspect of the soul which will determine whether or not another facet incarnates upon your world.

There are many in your world who don't want to be here now — is that right? There are many who don't want to leave your world, who want to spend forever here because they think that life is a bed of roses! There are some who are in the midst of so much suffering and pain that they cannot wait to leave, but these things are conditions of the mind and the body that influence the thinking. It is the soul that ultimately chooses what is best and what is right for its own progress."

Donna: "Do the higher spirits always exist in your world? Do they ever come back to earth?" Do you get to a stage where you have reached a certain unfolding and through your knowledge and self development, then you just exist in the spirit world?"

White Feather: "That is so. The roundabout of life that takes in the physical world is not an endless one. It may seem that you are going round and round but there will come a point when you step off, not to step back on again. When that time comes you will know that this earthly plane has served you well and has offered up all of the lessons and experiences that you needed to know and your soul has equipped itself well from these. That will be a glorious time for then you will know that you will continue in an unbroken sequence in the spiritual realms of life in which many wonderful things await you. Much joy and happiness will be there for you.

When I see a soul born in your world I am sometimes filled with sadness. When you have a baby born in your world you are overjoyed, you are happy — a new soul has come upon the earth and you cry tears of joy. In my world we cry tears of sadness because we know what that soul has to undergo. So when we welcome back finally, that soul, having fulfilled through many lifetimes of endless struggle and see it experience the true awareness of the divinity that lies within it, then again we cry – tears of happiness, because we know that the glorious pathway of light, into the realms of spiritual unfoldment, await it."

It had been a long but fulfilling evening and as the sitting drew to a close it was evident that Donna's first encounter with White Feather had been a rewarding one. But there was still one more question to come, from Amanda:

Amanda: "Can I just ask one final thing White Feather......if on a personal level one has an inkling that someone may be in the last couple of years of their life, is that something that we may be permitted to know? Or is it purely a human concern?"

White Feather: "No, no....you have earned the right to know it. When you develop spiritually your perception, your ability to perceive things beyond the five senses of physical matter, increases. It is.....I was going to say, a 'by-product' of spiritual growth and unfoldment, but it is much more than that. It is a core aspect of who and what you are because you see beyond the limits of material space and time. You see beyond and through matter as you become more aware through a non-physical means, of information that you would otherwise not have access to. Let me add something most important to that Sunflower; were you not spiritually strong enough to know it, then you would not become aware of it. Always remember that. When in your moments of sadness and weakness perhaps, you think to yourself 'this is more than I can bear, I don't want to know this' and you know that a certain sequence will lead to a particular outcome, stop, pause, look at yourself and remind yourself that you only know this information because your soul has equipped itself with the means to be aware of it. That should give you a crumb of comfort because it means that you are spiritually strong enough, that you have the growth that enables you to deal with it. Do you see what I am saying?"

Amanda: "So what I am feeling at the moment is true?"

White Feather: "It is true."

Amanda: "We'll bring things to a close now and I'd like to thank you very much White Feather for linking with us. It's a privilege and a pleasure to have you here to speak to us and for us to have the benefit of your knowledge and wisdom and for all those in spirit that stand at your side."

Donna: "Yes thank you White Feather, it really has been very enlightening for us."

White Feather: "It is very nice to be able to address you, interact with you, and communicate with you in this way and the privilege as always, is mine, because it is always a delight to serve. There is no greater privilege than to serve and help others. I have helped you tonight but I know without question that you will help others."

Sensing that the very personal question that Amanda had asked regarding a loved one and which the guide had answered so honestly had touched her deeply, White Feather added a final

few words of comfort, bringing the mammoth session to a close with a gentle and poignant reminder:

White Feather: "Sunflower…..the tears that fill your eyes….let us wipe them away, for you will know and understand in the fullness of time the great joy that is to be found in the reality of the continuity of life. Even though physical changes come about, even though our loved ones may depart from us, always the ties of love will bind us together. Always remember this…..and I will finish with this…..that it is always darkest just before the dawn. In the darkest of nights, the sun is still shining, the stars are still in the heavens, the wind still blows, the flowers still grow, all is as it should be because the Great Spirit knows all and is all, and all is understood and all is known and all will be safely gathered in. No one will ever be lost or forgotten or left alone. The ones who are filled with sadness will be uplifted. The ones who are filled with ignorance will be given knowledge. Those who walk in darkness and fear will be given light and will be showered with love and understanding. Always remember these things. You are richly loved and looked upon with great, great delight because you are all facets of the Great White Spirit. You and I, though we are different, we are the same, though we are apart, we are together, though we are individuals, we are one.

May I take my leave and as I do so, once again reiterate the great love that we have. I hope that we can repeat this communication once again at some point in the future. We thank you all, not only those of you here in this temple but the many who gather in my world to participate in these proceedings. Thank you all and may the power and love of the Great Spirit be forever at your side."

"You as a total individual vibrate at a unique frequency"

Five

Resonance

Some readers will know that in scientific language, resonance is the tendency of a system to oscillate at maximum amplitude at a certain frequency - a term commonly known as the system's resonant frequency. White Feather, who is known for his ability to combine scientific and esoteric wisdom took this as his main theme during a communication that was truly inspirational. Opening his talk by establishing a link between resonance and the attunement of guide and medium, he quickly broadened his philosophy to encompass a more profound teaching with far reaching implications:

White Feather: "I link with you tonight as I have done so often, on the vibration of love. That we are able to share a commonality through attunement is the result of a resonance that exists between us. It is often stated that 'like attracts like' and that is a supreme universal truth for there has to be a common thread operating between instrument and guide to enable the intimate flow of energy to obtain, sufficient for us to impart that which we seek to give.

Everything, as I have said so often, is energy. Whether to you it appears transparent or whether it offers the illusion of solidity, it is still energy. Energy is movement and within the energy of movement is vibration and resonance. It is about resonance that I wish to speak to you this night for it is a key element for all of life's transactions. For at whatever level of existence you find yourself at any point in time and space, you can be assured that you are involved in many exchanges of energy upon numerous levels. Those of you who are aware of the quantum fields will know that nothing is separate from anything and that at the deepest levels of being, all is connected as one.

In the quantum world the laws of Newtonian physics do not apply. Time and space are obliterated and they are replaced by the simple yet profound truth – I AM. For all things are of the Great Spirit and there is nothing that is outside, apart from or separate from the Great Spirit. Spirit is timeless, formless, infinite and it comes into matter, into and through form in order to express itself and reveal its latent divinity. At all points, at all moments along the pathway there are exchanges of energy and force upon innumerable levels of being.

What do we mean by 'exchanges of energy?' Perhaps the simplest analogy I can offer is the application of heat, to water. Here the exchange of energy transforms the structure of water and turns it into steam. As the water evaporates, its molecules quicken and its state changes from liquid to gas.

But what of energy exchanges in which you partake? Exchanges upon a physical level, you may already be aware of. For example; when you ride a bicycle, the effort exerted by your limbs upon the pedals, enable the wheels to turn. This application provides the energy for the bike to move. You know, all of you who are musicians, that if you strike a tuning fork it will resonate with a particular note or even another object in the room. The distance involved does not prevent the vibration or sound from travelling through the air and resonating with something that lies a little distance away. But what I am more interested in teaching about in this communication, is the resonance of you as an individual, with others who come into the orbit of your life and with various places and circumstances with which you come into contact."

The guide went on to explain how every individual is unique and could never, under any circumstances be copied - a teaching that flies in the face of some who believe that both animals and humans can be cloned in totality:

"You as a total individual, vibrate at a unique frequency. This is not replicated exactly anywhere in the universe. It is your unique signature. This frequency of vibration, this resonance belongs solely to you. Others may come close, but they are not the same. You carry this frequency which has many facets, including sound and colour wherever you go. As you move through life you do so within various energy fields – physical, emotional, mental and spiritual. The physical energy fields we have touched upon briefly and I don't want to elaborate upon them on this occasion. What is of greater import are the fields of mind and emotion in which you move.

At this moment in time in your incarnation upon the earth, you have acquired a personality which is the result of your genetic predisposition and this determines to a degree, your thoughts, your motives, your interests, your actions and your words combined with the individual you that is the result of all that you have ever been and

and all that you are. This combination provides the unique signature and imprint that you leave upon life. Now, if you are upon the pathway of unfoldment, if your evolution has taken you to the heights of spiritual awareness, then you will resonate with like minds in my world and yours and also be drawn to various circumstances and events and experiences that are in harmony with that which you resonate.

Magnetically you will be drawn to and will attract these circumstances. Equally, you will repel others which have no value to you and can offer you little or nothing in the way of true experience.

The more evolved you are, the more powerful you become and the more you are able to resist the energies of lower minds and indeed your own ego state. So in that sense life becomes easier, more comfortable and more spiritual. Your frequency is quickened and you resonate at a higher level.

Those who have yet to understand the true nature of their being and who live their lives still adhering to form and to matter and become attached to the lower base states will find that they resonate at lower frequencies and so draw to themselves events, circumstances and experiences that prove more difficult and yet still offer them the necessary experience to equip themselves for learning and spiritual growth."

Many of us have had the experience of being able to sense something about an individual or place and often this is referred to as the 'sixth sense'. As the spirit teacher continued with his philosophy he seemed to be hinting that this ability is indeed attributable to the vibrational signature that we each possess:

"You will find that sometimes you are in circumstances where you come in to contact with those who resonate at a more gross frequency. If you are not sufficiently developed yourself, to be aware of them, you may find that their energies impact upon yours and they will draw from you. Consciously, you may be unaware of this. Unconsciously you may know and instinctively feel uncomfortable. How often have you been in the presence of others and you are not happy in their midst? You feel a repulsion that you cannot quite explain and you wish to remove yourself from their presence. They may not have said or have done anything to hurt you or dissuade you and yet on a deeper level there is a knowing that you are not of their vibration. Equally, you will find that you are attracted to those who perhaps, you meet for the first time, and it seems that almost immediately you are in synchronisation with their thought processes and their emotional aspect. It is as if you have known them for years. In some instances you have - for many lifetimes.

What is happening here is that you are resonating. Your aura and their aura are combining and there is no discord. Like gears meshing together in some great machine, they blend effortlessly into one motion and the exchange of energy is harmonious.

Try to understand that the vibrations of the higher spiritual aspects are much, much swifter, much finer than the slower, coarser vibrations of the lower states and emotions. Love for example, is a much quicker more refined energy than hatred. Truth carries its own light and its own frequency, whereas those who lie and cheat and deceive, whose lives are filled with ignorance and darkness, vibrate upon a much coarser, slower frequency.

You must surely have found yourself at times, entering into a building or house for the first time and sensing the energies of that place? How often have you said to yourself 'I feel at home here, this place has a nice feel about it?' Equally, you may have been in circumstances where you felt the opposite and felt quite uncomfortable. Perhaps here you are picking up residual energies that still resonate from past events.

So you have to understand and realise that you move within an ocean of frequencies. Nothing is strictly as it appears, certainly not in a physical sense. If you are able to see from a different vantage point you will observe the physical universe to be a mass of swirling energies, colours, vibrations, electrons, protons, neutrons and sub-atomic particles creating ripples upon the fabric of space and time. It is the physical brain and the mind and consciousness that operates through it that deciphers these frequencies and transforms them into what you think is reality. What you have to understand and to a great extent avoid, is buying into that 'reality' and becoming attached to it. You have to learn the art of non-attachment, of moving to higher frequencies. Realise that it is within the formless, timeless, boundless worlds that your true state of being exists. This of matter - these confining lowering vibrations, deceive you, seek to capture you and hold you fast. With the aid of the ego, the lower states of mind and emotion would seek to throw a net over the fast beating wings of your higher spirit that seeks to soar unto the heights of freedom."

Reiterating that we are all 'beings of light' at the essential level, White Feather brought his talk to its conclusion with an upbeat message that applies to every soul, regardless of their status in life:

"By all means live your life in the world of matter. Enjoy your time upon the physical worlds that you inhabit, but do not under any circumstances believe that this is your true home – it is not. Like feet which step across the stones that cross the river of life, so you set foot upon worlds that offer you something from which your soul can learn and equip itself and quicken. The worlds of matter are but stepping stones and when you have learned all of life's lessons you begin to resonate to the song of the spirit and this most glorious of music, when it plays upon the strings of your heart, will resonate in all the chambers of your form. You will be transformed.

I sometimes hear it said that man is a 'being of light'. The term 'light worker' is one that is used commonly I think, in your culture today. There is some truth in that, for in essence you are light. Spirit is light. Where there is true spiritual unfoldment, you will always find there is light. Where there is light, there is no darkness - just as where there is truth, there is no ignorance.

Seek always to bring harmony in your dealings with others. Pay respect to every form of life, however insignificant you consider it to be. It has a right to be there and its place in the universe is on an equal footing with your own. Seek always to serve, for service is the coin of the spirit. It is through service that you are served. It is through giving that you receive and in this way progress is inevitable. Remember that you are not your form. You are not your place of work, you are not your title - you are not even your gender. You are not your personality. You are an individual and that individual is part of the Great Spirit, which is infinite. May the light and the truth of the Great Spirit be with you all. God bless."

Demonstrating his consistency in adhering to the pool of knowledge and wisdom from which he draws his answers the

spirit ambassador had, several months earlier been asked a question that had been emailed to his medium, asking if the guide could respond at the next available sitting. The question concerned the very nature of spirit and energy, questioning if they were one and the same thing. This is what White Feather said:

"In truth ALL energy is spirit, for ALL THINGS are spirit. Indeed, what is matter if not a condensed form of spirit? Whatever terminology you choose to employ, the truth is that energy, of whatever form, is animated, as are all facets of creation by the power of the spirit. Perhaps the real question should be 'what is the Spirit?' Certainly it would be over simplistic to assert that spirit is energy or that energy is spirit, for that establishes very little in concrete terms and only addresses semantics. To me, Spirit is the One Essence, the First Cause and All that is. I refer to this essence as the Great Spirit or God, but to define this in terms of language is indeed very difficult as words, which do indeed often cloak our thoughts, are inadequate to convey the infinite. Let us for simplicity sake, state that the Great Spirit was, is and always shall be. The energy, force and intelligence that animates creation and manifests through multitudinous forms is not the totality of the divine source, only a facet of it, just as the breath is not the body, or the thought, the man. In essence, neither does the creator evolve, for it is already perfected. What does evolve is its expression through the vehicles of matter and its higher bodies that enable more of its perfection to be realised."

Through the wonders of modern technology, the guide's answer was carefully typed out verbatim and emailed back to the originator. If nothing else, the internet provides a way to reach souls who might otherwise not have the opportunity of gaining access to certain areas of information.

That White Feathers' words may have reached someone whom he has never met in person will have pleased him, as his work is all about 'touching souls'. Ultimately, it matters not what form of delivery is used, so long as the message is imparted and the needs of the recipient addressed. For even though all of life is connected, the guide himself would surely agree, perhaps with a wry smile, that a helping hand from the world of matter is occasionally welcome.

"Each question deserves an answer"

Six

The abundant stream

One of the most exciting features of any White Feather communication, especially one that takes place in a public setting is listening to him dispatch wisdom in answering an often diverse range of questions of which he has no prior knowledge. His replies are often profound and instant, delivered without a moments hesitation - the hallmark of a wise sage. Here, we include a random selection taken from various demonstrations which illustrate how the spirit teacher utilises his spiritual knowledge, compassion and understanding to help those seeking an explanation to some of life's many mysteries:

Q: "Given that matter is subservient to spirit, could you explain to us the purpose and spiritual significance of black holes which scientists have discovered throughout the universe?"

White Feather: "How long have you got?" [audience laughter}

Questioner: "As long as you can give us please!"

White Feather: "Talking here on a scientific level, I will try and simplify it when I say that black holes in your universe are white holes in other universes – they are connecting vortexes in that they take matter from one universe in a physical sense and they recycle it into another. You will find in the nature of your world that all matter and all energy is recycled. No energy is capable of being destroyed. All energy is indestructible - it changes its state from one to another.

In the simple case of the physical body, when the spirit withdraws and the body decays, the energy is taken back into the physical form of the earth and reconstituted and reborn into new forms. The purpose, or one of the purposes of black holes in the universe is actually to cleanse it and recycle matter and give it birth into another frequency. You have to understand – and your scientists have not discovered this yet, that your universe, which they think is everything, is only one of countless universes, each upon its own level or frequency of vibration. So to answer the question in the simplest way possible, that is what black holes constitute."

Q: *"You've touched lightly on the ego, can this aspect of the individual interfere in the operation of mediumship?"*

White Feather: "It can indeed son, which is why I spoke of it tonight. Certainly as far as mediumship is concerned where you have an ego, then you have problematic events which sometimes cannot be overcome easily - where you have mediums who, when they begin to develop their gifts and operate in the public arena can allow their ego to interfere and this has a way of blocking the frequency and the subtlety of the energies and thought processes that we have to impart. You know we have said that we have to bypass the conscious mind and the ego has a way of interfering and cutting in. It is rather like you trying to talk to someone and another voice keeps butting in saying 'ah, but it has to be this way' or 'this is the way....hear me'. This is what the ego does. The ego is not all bad - please don't misunderstand. There has to be a certain amount of ego and you have to understand that it is that positive aspect of it that gives individuals the impetus and the confidence to stand and work in public, otherwise they would not be able to do that. But it is where there is an overemphasis of ego and it thinks that it is more important than anything else and it grabs attention for itself. It will go to great lengths to do that, even to the point of creating chaos in one's material life to get attention and you may have sometimes heard the term 'poor me' – one who has all the problems in the world and yet seems to relish and revel in those problems because attention is drawn. It is very often the ego that is creating this scenario and this is only one way in which it works. You have those who have such an inflated opinion of themselves that they think they are above everyone else, they are so important! Mediumship cannot operate and function correctly and as freely as it should and so this is why I always emphasise that any aspiring medium should keep their feet upon the ground. Indeed, any of you – keep your head in the clouds but keep your feet upon the ground."

Very often White Feather is asked questions concerning mediumship, particularly by those concerned with their own development. Here, a lady enquires of the guide whether or not his medium has any recollection of what has been spoken through him, bringing a somewhat humorous response from the spirit control:

White Feather: "He has some recollection afterwards, although this is fragmented. So I can talk about him, and very often do! *[audience laughter]* In all seriousness, because I am operating through an aspect of the mind that is not immediately available to his consciousness. Much of what I say is lost to him, but fragments of it do pop up into his consciousness later and he does have some limited recall of them."

Q: "When you draw close to the vessel that you work with, do you use his energy or do you use energy from the people sitting in front of you?"

White Feather: "I do both. Some of you may notice that you have developed a tickle in your throat, a little cough perhaps, because energy is taken - with your higher souls' permission, from all of you. We do not take energy from those whose energy levels are depleted but some of you have a greater abundance of energy and so we draw from you. We also draw from the medium's own energy levels.
Sometimes when we work through instruments we even take energy from the curtains, the carpets, the furniture, from the chairs and other things that we can utilise because everything in essence is energy. There is nothing which is not energy. In fact if you were to use, let us say a certain chair in a physical circle for a number of years, you would find that eventually the chair would fall apart because we had taken so much energy from it that it's structure would be transformed! So we have to be careful what we take, but we also give back a little, we don't leave you short."

Q: "Thank you."

White Feather: "You are interested in trance aren't you?"

Questioner: "I am trying to develop at the moment and I get very low energy and also my carpet has gone funny at home!"

White Feather: "Yes.....we can't take the blame for that! But regarding your energy, you have to understand that trance mediumship and in particular, deeper levels of trance bordering upon what you call physical mediumship utilise the employment of the endocrine system and this can have an impact upon the physical body and upon its glucose and sugar levels and the energy levels in total. Sometimes you find that some physical mediums, if sufficient care is not taken can, in later life develop diabetes as a result of over use of their gift. So we have to be very careful. There will be some depletion but we do give energy back and your energy levels will return. We do not do anything to knowingly endanger a medium. The best advice that I can give you is to have an intake of sugar, a sugary substance to raise your glucose levels after sitting if you are able to do that."

Question: "White Feather, have you an opinion on table tilting?"

White Feather: "I have an opinion on a lot of things! Table tilting, which again falls within the auspices of physical mediumship can be a useful tool. I don't think however, that it is as high up the scale of spiritual expression as true trance mediumship, where philosophy can be imparted, but it has its place as do other aspects of physical mediumship such as table rapping and other phenomena. It is useful.....it is not the ultimate means to an end, but if there are those mediums who have potential and whose energies can be used by those in my world to move the table, or rap the table then it is good to pursue it. All mediumship if it is undertaken with the highest motives and principles, and allows the truth of the spirit and life after death to be made manifest unto mankind, is in my view worthy, but I would always aim for the higher. It is a starting point but one should always seek to move to higher things."

Q: "Sometimes I walk down my room and the remote control moves and switches on the television. Now I would like to believe that it is someone from spirit but is it that or is it my own energy that is causing it to happen?"

White Feather: "It can be either. I suspect, looking at you that it is from you because some individuals, some mediums create a very powerful energy around themselves – an aura of energy and electronic objects in particular can respond to it. I know of many mediums who cannot wear a watch. They cannot walk into a room without an object moving as you have described, because they have this energy field around them. I wouldn't be too perturbed about it. Don't worry or be concerned about it. Just acknowledge it and recognise that it is part of the energy field that you have."

Questioner: "How can we develop our gifts?"

White Feather: "Well as in all things it is a matter of discipline, motive and practice. When you were a child you had to learn to walk. You fell over many times but you picked yourself up again. You had to learn to ride a bike and to swim. You had to learn to speak and to do many things and you did this over a period of time through trial and error, through observation, through practice, through dedication, by making mistakes and through this, you acquired those attributes. Those attributes that you found so difficult, once you had acquired them, became unconscious. You do them without thinking and it is the same with mediumship – you have to learn through dedication, through the right intention, the right motive, to serve, to develop the gifts that you have. You may not be able to develop them easily if they are buried deeply within you, but all can serve, let me say that. *All* can serve.

What is service anyway? It is not standing upon the platform giving clairvoyant messages or delivering philosophy, it's holding out a hand to someone who needs it and saying a quiet word to someone who is suffering. It is helping the soul who is in difficulty. It is giving kindness or a gentle touch to those that need it. That is real service. Sometimes that service is not undertaken in the gaze of the spotlight but in the quietness of the sanctuary or in the stillness of the field. It doesn't matter where it's given as long as you give service. Service is the coin of the spirit. Service is the coin that enables you to receive. If you give freely and if you seek knowledge and truth and your motive is right, then it will be drawn to you. Always remember that. No one ever asks and is turned away. If you ask and if you seek, it will be given."

Q: *"Sometimes I've had messages about things around me, my house, my friends, my life, but very rarely do I get things about the future. Is this more difficult for you or is it not possible?"*

White Feather: "As I said to my friend here, the greater the spiritual development and psychic ability, the farther that the medium is permitted to see future events. But sometimes you know, we don't always tell you what is coming because it is not always wise to do so. If you knew everything that was on your pathway, then it is human nature that there would be some things that you would seek to avoid. Is that not so? You would say 'I don't want to experience that, I'm going to go this way!' But in choosing that, you may miss out on a very valuable lesson. That is why at this level of being you specifically are not aware of everything that is to come upon your pathway. Not only that, but not everything is pre-determined. You have your freewill and that has to be taken into account, because your freewill determines what happens to a large extent, in the future. It's not always necessary or wise that you know future events because it will prevent you from learning the many lessons that you have come here to learn."

As mentioned previously, often during live trance events the spirit helpers will draw energy from some of those present. This is not in any way harmful but occasionally results in certain individuals coughing. Having received an apology from the guide, a lady who appeared to be experiencing discomfort responded with a question concerning an aspect of mediumship that can also affect the throat area:

White Feather: "How is your cough? I'm sorry if we are taking a little energy from you. You will need a drink of water perhaps?"

Q: "Can I ask….I've seen someone transfigured more than once and sometimes the whole person disappears. Can you tell me how or why this happens?"

White Feather: "Because we build an ectoplasmic mask in front of the medium. In true transfiguration we build an ectoplasmic mask which enables the incoming spirit to manifest, to step into that mask and to mould that mask to their appearance so that their form overshadows that of the medium. It's rather like one person standing in front of another and the medium disappears because they are obscured by the vision that has transposed itself over them."

Questioner: "It wasn't the medium, it was someone else. It wasn't done intentionally."

White Feather: "Yes, but I beg to differ. There is still an aspect of mediumship present, even if they are aware of it or not. They may not know they are a medium, but there has to be some aspect of mediumship involved in order for the energies to be used. Some people are mediums and they never know it!
There are some surgeons you know, who perform operations in your world, whose hands are guided by the unseen hands of spirit helpers and they don't even know it! They go through their whole lives performing operations and they don't know how much they are helped from my world. Fact!"

Q: "Is it the spirit world who actually decide whether you do trance or transfiguration?"

White Feather: "There are a number of factors, but primarily it depends upon your constitution — that is the make up of your physical and etheric bodies. You will find that those who are true mediums have come here [earth] because that is their work in this lifetime. They have agreed from a soul level to undertake this work and so they choose the vehicle, the physical body that will enable their mediumship to develop. It's no good saying 'I'm going to live the life of a medium' and then coming into a body that has no aspects that can be utilised for mediumship. So the vehicle has to be selected through the parentage very, very precisely and distinctly and that vehicle, that vessel, that body, has a leaning towards mediumship. Its constitution is such that mediumship can develop and you find that very often deep trance mediums, transfiguration mediums, physical mediums, have an abundance of ectoplasm. It is there to be used, by the spirit. Those who don't have an abundance of ectoplasm could never be a physical medium if they tried their whole lifetime. It wouldn't happen!

So as far as whose decision it is; it is the soul of the incoming spirit who comes through that form, that decides that it is going to undertake that work, that initiates that vessel, the vehicle to be born so that at some later date in life its qualities can be developed and used in the name of mediumship."

Q: "I came into spiritualism at the age of twenty and I was given three names of guides who worked with me, then I had a period when I could not work spiritually. Now I have begun to do so again and I wondered if those same guides would still be with me?"

White Feather: "Not necessarily. You will find that very often guides are with you, some for a complete life span - those who work closely with you, and others who come for a certain time to do their work and then withdraw. So everyone is different. I cannot guarantee that if you were given three names, that they will continue to be with you, although it is equally possible that they will.

So it depends on the circumstances of why you withdrew from that pathway and whether or not when you return you have work to pick up, to pick up the reins again. I suspect that if that is the case then those who were drawn to you initially will still be part of your soul group and will again seek to work with you."

Readers familiar with White Feather's philosophy will know that the guide often speaks about reincarnation, sometimes in the face of opposition. Here a member of the audience asks the guide if individuals are compelled to return to the earth, a question which initially draws a comical reply followed by a deeper response from the sage:

Q: "Do we have to reincarnate upon earth…..are we forced to do so?"

White Feather: "Do I sense that you don't want to?…!!"

Questioner: "Well……"

White Feather: "You have a choice, but it is a limited choice in some aspects. Your freewill still operates but there will come a point where you realise that unless you put right what you have done wrong, unless you outwork karmic laws or 'balance the books' if I may put it that way, then you cannot progress further in my world. The Great Spirit isn't going to stand over you with a stick and demand that you return – that will come from in here *[the guide pointed to his chest]* and when that realisation dawns there are no hard and fast rules in terms of time, your soul will make the decision for you, to return perhaps to this world."

Questioner: *"And can we choose the parents that we want to come to?"*

White Feather: "Yes, again, where you have a degree of unfoldment then you have earned the right to choose the vehicle through which you come and your parentage. Some find that they have not earned that right and their return or re-entry into the body of matter is more automatic, but where you have evolved spiritually then you will choose that line of decent and your parentage because you will know that it will equip your soul with the necessary means to outwork and achieve whatever it comes to do."

Q: *"If we reincarnate and come back to earth in a new body, do we have to start again from scratch?"*

White Feather: "No, you don't have to start from scratch. You take forward what you learn from one life into another and if it is that you make the choice to return to the world of substance and reincarnate into matter then you don't have to start over again. You have to learn the ABC, you have to learn the arithmetic, you have to learn to walk, you have to learn to eat and all of the other things that go with that particular culture, but you bring with you the gathered, collected wisdom that you have accumulated from past lives. This is how progress is made. You may not always be aware of it consciously, but it is there, inherent within your thoughts and actions and that is why it comes to its fruition, particularly when you reach puberty and you find that the higher soul aspect can begin to influence your actions and thoughts.

Of course, there are exceptions. You have some child prodigies don't you in your world? You have the Mozart's of your world and others - great thinkers, great musicians and artists who can demonstrate from a very young age their true wisdom. They are old souls. This will always be the case and will always be demonstrated. So in answer to your question; yes, you take with you, your accumulation into the next phase of life."

On another occasion a question arose concerning the length of time spent upon earth and whether or not reincarnating for a brief time is actually worthwhile:

Q: *"We are told within Spiritualism that we can, if we want to, return to the earth and carry on with our learning. This we understand, but what I can't understand is; how come children of such a young age go back to spirit, or they are even taken whilst they are still in the mother's womb? What actually have they learned if they go back so soon?"*

White Feather: "By what yardstick do you measure learning? By what physical means do you measure learning? It is not the length of time that you are in the body, it is what is learned through the experience. You can be in a physical body for seventy, eighty, ninety, a hundred years and learn very little. You can touch upon this earth and pass back into my world prematurely – in the physical sense, and yet you have fulfilled your life's purpose. You have to look, not with the eyes of matter, but with the eyes of the spirit and make your judgement based upon that principle, because it's not how long you are here, but what you learn through the experience.

I know of many who have come to your world and they have lived but a few hours in the physical body, or perhaps a few years and then they returned to their true home in the spirit world, but they outworked their Karma. They came for a purpose and the body and the experience served them well. Others have lived for over ninety years and they have gone backwards in a sense – they have learned nothing. So you cannot look and measure with the eyes of matter, you have to look with the eyes of the spirit."

Q: "Can you explain to us why God allows a young child to be killed in an accident? It seems so cruel that any parent should have to suffer this. How does this equate with an all loving God?"

White Feather: "Well first of all there are no 'accidents' because all is operating through natural law. As for it being cruel I understand your concern and when you look at it from one perspective it does seem cruel that a mother should lose a child., but you have to look with the eyes of the spirit. When you look from one perspective you see one thing. When you are down in the valley and you see an event occur, you judge it from that perspective. When you stand upon the highest mountain and look down you see it from a different perspective. What to you is heartache and despair and sorrow at of the loss of a loved one, what to you is a defeat, many be a victory to the spirit. Because in the greater scheme of life a deeper lesson has been learned, not only by the one who has passed but also by the one left behind – and I use that term very loosely, because where there is love there is no separation.

So try and look if you can, beyond the tears, beyond the heartache, beyond the pain and see the greater lesson, the greater reason behind all things that happen - chance and fate do not occur in an ordered universe, always remember that."

Q: *"How will we see our loved ones when we ourselves pass over? Will we see them as physical bodies?"*

White Feather: "Yes, more often than not you will see their physical body and you will see them as you recognise them, not as they might have been at the time of their passing but as you would recognise them. You have to understand that. What would be the point of one in my world appearing to you if there was no recognition? You must understand that our world is very ordered, things don't happen by chance. For example, let us say for the purposes of illustration that you lost a child - twenty, thirty, forty years have elapsed, you have grown older in the physical sense upon the earth and your child has grown in my world and matured. When you pass you will perhaps hope that and expect to see the child you knew when it passed and that will be the case. Over a period of time when you adjust in my world, that individual will reveal themself to you in their changed state, their state of growth. Because growth still occurs in my world and we reach maturity in the spiritual sense, so we have to take these things into account."

Q: *"How do you explain to someone who passes over that they are dead and have to move on?"*

White Feather: "Well that is a very good question and there are those in my world who do not realise that they are dead! They don't realise it or they don't want to realise it and it can take some period of time before they do realise it. But when they are shown certain things then realisation dawns on them and they have to come to face what has happened. If they don't then they may find themselves temporarily trapped in the realms closest to your world, which is why you have all manner of things like hauntings and disturbances where souls don't want to move on because they are so attached to their earthly life. We have to try and help them, sometimes with the help of those in your world to make them see that they are indeed no longer in the physical dimension."

Questioner: "Do you only help young ones, who have no idea what has happened to them?"

White Feather: "No we help all. We do not discriminate and after all what is a young one? A young one may be an old soul. We do not discriminate between old and young, we help all who need help, who are able to receive it."

Q: "You often hear about levels in the spirit world, how many levels are there?"

White Feather: "I don't know, I haven't counted them! I know that this book will say there are nine, that one will say there are seven, another will say there are fourteen, but who has counted them? You tell me? What I always say to people is that there are successive realms going higher in frequency and refinement and there are realms going lower, descending into darkness. As souls continue to unfold, the realm at which they can vibrate is available to them. You must understand that the spirit life is infinite and I know of no finality. You do not reach the top of the ladder. I know of no one who has got to the highest realm and has come back to speak of it because always they say that there is more, life is eternal. Perfection is reached only in eternity, so as the refinement continues, the realms appear.

You have to understand that the realms in my world correspond to the consciousness of those who inhabit them, the greater the expression of spirit, the greater the light, the greater the realm itself - the level is created by those that inhabit it."

Q: "Here on earth we have twenty-four hours in a day and each day we age, we get older. Do people get older in the spirit world?"

White Feather: "You don't age in the sense that you age in the physical world, where things grow and then decay and eventually die, but there is change of sorts. Time you know, does pass in my world but not in the sense that you would understand it. I have heard it said that 'there is no time', well that is not strictly true. It depends upon what level you exist. The higher you go in terms of spiritual development, the less that time seems to pass and you are entering into realms where past, present and future merge together into one. The closer you get to the earth plane the more that time seems to be pronounced. I am aware, at the level at which I operate, of the passage of time. I can remember when I first started to link with this medium, some thirty-five years or so ago, so I am aware of the passing of time. There are others around me who speak of the past and talk of the future, but in your world time is more linear. In my world it is more rounded and the sense of time is different. It is sensed differently, there is a different awareness of the passage of time - that is the easiest way to describe it to you.

As for the soul - it changes and evolves and you reach the pinnacle of what you would have been upon the earth. There can be a difference in appearance – there are some in my world who appear with white hair, but they are not old. There are others who continue to operate as children and yet they are older souls than the ones with the white hair! So you see, it is a world of contrasts in that sense. It is a question of the level that you would have reached in your spiritual maturity had you continued to exist upon the earth. Appearance doesn't account for a great deal in the true nature of existence. It is what is within that counts."

Q: *"When we pass over to the next phase of life, what about the wars that have gone on and are still going on now, will they continue where we go to?"*

White Feather: "There are no wars in my world. The only conflict in my world lies within the minds of those who are upon the lower levels and you are not going there. The lower levels contain souls who have to face the consequences of their earthly actions and within them there is conflict and pain and suffering. It is not 'hell', but it is a state of their own making. In the normal sense you will find that the realms of light contain only harmony – no war, no conflict, no pain. So don't worry!"

Q: *"I want to know if there is any significance in the date of 2012. Will mankind move to another level of spiritual understanding?"*

White Feather: *"Well you know, I have heard this date given on many occasions and I wonder who arrived at that decision? It is rather like those who say there are a set number of planes in the spirit world – I always say 'who counted them?' You have to realise that there is a spiritual renaissance of sorts already taking place because man it is at a crossroads. There are certain elements in your world who are seeking to enslave humanity, to gain control and to turn the human race in to race of slaves who respond to their will. Equally there are many who are awakening to the divine aspect within as there always have been throughout history and the higher must always, eventually emerge triumphant because darkness cannot win over light. Ignorance cannot emerge supreme over understanding, wisdom and truth.

So there are many battles of sorts being fought at the moment, but I don't like to put deadlines upon them. Man measures time artificially. He divides it into periods of years and months and weeks and days and hours and seconds. Real time is a flow of energy, so there are, like the ocean, times when man ebbs and flows. There are periods of ignorance and there are periods where he advances. At the moment there are battles being fought to enable the higher, divine aspect to remain manifest in your world and despite what you read in your newspapers, the violence that you see on your news and all the gloom that is around you, there are many, many souls who are awakening and becoming aware of what is, what truly is, rather like the currents beneath the ocean. So do not despair because the truth will ultimately win through the day."

Q: "Is it true that before we come to the earth we actually make our pathway….you know, where we are going, the mistakes we are to make, that sort of thing?"

White Feather: "You have been to the earth plane many, many times.

As you walk along the pathway of life, you learn. You make mistakes, you stumble, you err, you fall, you learn, you gather momentum and you set into motion the law of cause and effect. Within every cause there is an effect and within every effect there is another cause and so you sow and reap as you pass through life. Some things you do in error, some things you do in knowledge. The greater the wisdom and spiritual development that you have, the greater the responsibility that comes with it. If you make mistakes, no one is going to judge you. If you do something and act from a higher state of knowledge and you know the responsibility that comes with it but you still make the mistake anyway, then there is a greater price to be paid.

So you are where you are today, all of you, because of what you did, you thought, you said, yesterday. You were yesterday, where you were, because of what you did before that! So everything is connected. You will find yourself in tomorrow's world, or in a thousand years from now where you are because of what you do now. You are the architects, the creators, no one else. You have to take full responsibility. So you make your own path."

Questions concerning our earth and the many changes that the planet is currently undergoing feature regularly during White Feather question and answer sessions, along with enquiries regarding the reasons for suffering. Here are a small selection beginning with one from a gentleman who wanted to know if God knew everything that was happening in the world:

Q: "In the book 'Conversations with God' it is stated that 'we are never alone, God is always with us'. Can we assume that this is God's way of knowing everything about us and suffering all of the things we suffer?"

White Feather: "You have to understand son......and that's a very good question by the way....that in simple terms the answer is yes, because you are God. The Great Spirit, or God is not some lofty soul who sits upon a throne overlooking your domain. You are God and God is within you. As you experience, so the Great Spirit or God is aware of it – there is no separation. As for God suffering, God doesn't suffer in that sense, but is aware of your suffering. The reason that you suffer is because you are imperfect, because you create conditions through your ignorance - and I am saying this in a loving way because we all are part of this pathway - you create suffering through ignorance. This brings about lessons that you have to learn and the Great Spirit or God, is aware of that because you are one with the Great Spirit.

If you think, for simplicity sake, of the Great Spirit as being in human form, then you could think of yourself and all others as being tiny cells contained within that body. Just as your body has cells, your bodily consciousness is aware of everything that is going on in your body.

You may not be, but there is an intelligence that is aware of it. Every cell that is born and dies, every tiny movement, every growth, every secretion, every intake – it is all known. So if you take that out unto the greater scale, because you are within God, the Great Spirit is aware of everything that happens.

Does it not say in your great book that 'when a sparrow falls from a tree, the Great Spirit is aware of it'? Does it not say that 'the very hairs upon your head are numbered'? – the Great Spirit knows. Trust the Great Spirit, harmonise and understand that the answers always lie within and that you will find them."

Q: "When I look around me I see a beautiful world that is being spoiled by ignorant minds who have no respect. I see people being killed, I see species becoming extinct, I see children growing up in poverty, who have no values and no concern for others around them…..when will God return this earth to a state of harmony and peace?"

White Feather: "I don't think your planet will ever be a Garden of Eden or a paradise. I would wish that it were, but it is after all, a place of learning. If it were perfect, if every aspect of it were light and love and harmony, then you would not learn the lessons of life. You come here into the material universe to learn lessons and of course one of those lessons is learning to respect the world in which you live and all the various life forms within it. That is part of the plan and if you do not do that, there are consequences not only to the planet and all forms upon it but also to you as individuals.

The short answer is; no, your world will never be perfect. It is not meant to be perfect. The lessons are there for the soul – the light and the dark, the good and the bad, the high and the low, the negative and the positive, all of these things which equip the soul for its ongoing journey. Do you see that?"

Questioner: "Yes I do."

White Feather: "I know that when you see life around you becoming extinct and you see beautiful species leaving the earth, your heart is filled with sadness. Mine is also, because I know that these creatures have taken many thousands, if not millions of years to evolve, but again as I said to earlier you have to look with the eyes of the spirit. Compensation and retribution are part of the spiritual law. Man has to face the consequence of his actions, both good and bad, negative and positive and all is known and understood. All will outwork itself in the fullness of time."

Q: *"Will we see the religions of the world uniting to give us peace upon this earth in our lifetime?"*

White Feather: "I think my dear friend, that peace comes not through religion but through the uniting of thoughts, minds and spirits. Religion is not a prerequisite for peace. I am not saying that peace cannot come through religion, but it is not necessary. Religion has been responsible for untold suffering and death and destruction upon your earth — why should it then yield peace? Even today wars are fought over religion, over dogma, over creed, over ceremony, over ancient texts and screeds and utterings that have been born largely out of the mind of man. A lot of spiritual truth has nothing to do with religion.
I would rather have you live in the garden of life than the cathedral of dogma. It is in the garden of life and experience that peace and happiness and unity are to be found. When man transcends dogma and creed and religion and he realises that his brother is as himself, that beneath the surface you are all parts of one great spiritual family then and only then, will peace come upon the earth. Not through division, not through creedalism, but by a realisation of the divine within."

"A gardener has to learn to let go of a flower. If he holds it tight, he crushes it."

Seven

Twist of the tale

When agreement was reached that a member of the UK police force would be afforded a sitting with White Feather the thinking behind it was that this would allow a unique opportunity to question the guide and seek his advice on how to tackle the ever increasing problem of crime and unrest.
However, sometimes things turn out quite differently than expected and when PC Mandy and her partner Richard came along to the specially arranged sitting it soon became evident that this would not be the session that was originally envisaged. Strangely, the guide displayed an unusual hesitancy when finally commencing his opening address by informing Amanda that he had initialised certain procedures before entrancing his medium:

White Feather: "Sunflower.....you are ahead of me. I wish to ensure that the necessary precautions are put in place for there are many of you here this night – not only all of you in the physical form but also many on my side of life."

After giving his opening speech the guide touched upon the many difficulties that seem to arise in modern society and how aggression seems to be so prevalent:

White Feather:"I do not want to elaborate too much in the first instance, for I wish to give you plenty, indeed ample opportunity to ask questions, but I thought I would just say a few words about the activities that many of you here are engaged in, in your daily lives. These often take you into situations in which you find hostility and difficulty from others in your world. There are many forms of aggression – it can be mental, it can be emotional, it can be physical, but all of it impacts upon your state of mind and wellbeing. Essentially, in spite of your training, it still has a bearing upon your day and you have to deal with it don't you? This time can be very debilitating; it can affect your whole way of thinking and being. The causes of the many forms of disquiet that are now manifesting in your world are multitudinous and I cannot simply dwell upon one cause, one reason. There has been a shift over recent times in that many of the souls who are now coming into your world are influenced by their peers in a negative way. There has been an erosion of values, of morals and this has had dire consequences in the way that society is shaped and moulded. It seems that there is little respect for others. It seems there is little regard for the laws of the land and for the wellbeing of everyone that combines to make up the culture in which are living. But you have to understand that this is the situation that has developed and you have to deal with it – but how to deal with it? This is the question; how do you respond? Do you merely follow the training that you have been given, that you have learned, that which you have acquired and developed? Or do you aspire to use your inner spiritual knowledge and wisdom and apply it where possible to the varying circumstances in which you find yourself daily?

There are two aspects here that I want to touch upon briefly; the first concerns changes in the cause of the effect – for everything has a cause and everything has an effect. You, because you are largely at the cutting edge and have to deal frequently with the effect and have to deal in an ongoing way, with the attacks, the language, the actions and the deeds of those who are the perpetrators of the current trend and you have to respond accordingly to your training. But if you can also apply your own spiritual understanding and try to act in accordance with the higher ideals which you each have then you are bringing an added dimension to the way that you deal with these situations.

If you can understand for example that many who are the perpetrators of disquiet in your world are themselves in a state of unease. They are ignorant in many regards and they are also in a state of agitation, their vibrations are not as they should be and you would do well to recognise that where their actions have a direct consequence to your wellbeing and those around you, they are not always acting in accordance with their true self. For they have been heavily influenced by events, by education or the lack of it, and by circumstances relating to their upbringing, by their immediate family and by a general disregard that has been cultured in modern society. So if you can bring the spiritual dimension to your work, albeit in a small way, then you are beginning to see things differently – you are beginning to work outside of the conditioned 'norm' to which many of your compatriots are expected to conform.

Secondly, there is a greater impact; a greater cause behind the effect and that can only be changed by education. By bringing understanding and awareness to these souls from a young age, by changing the ways of your schooling and education and by applying the spiritual truth in all that is taught. It is one thing to educate souls into reading and writing, into learning this and that about history, religion and science, but it is quite another to teach spiritual guidance, to help them to learn true spiritual lessons. If that were possible, then it would shape and change society and bring about a more enlightened state. Thus, the actions that are later perpetrated would not be so, for these actions of violence are born out of ignorance and not knowledge – not out of spiritual understanding.

If you can shape the young mind then you can change the adult. This should be the way forward. There are no easy solutions and I offer you not a complete answer to everything, for that is beyond me. I can only offer you the wisdom of those in my world who can see things from a different perspective and who can recognise the mistakes that man, collectively, is making in his attempts to bring about an organised and controlled society.

If you look at the bigger picture, if you go beyond the individual and look at world events you will see that the same patterns are being painted, the same mistakes are being made over and over again. Man thinks that he can bring about peace through violent means. If you sow the seeds of destruction you reap a harvest of unrest and further destruction. If you want peace, then you have to sow peace. Man cannot gain peace through war and destruction. He thinks that he can and the powers that be seek to influence those malleable, pliable minds into following their creed and dogma. But it has failed and it will continue to fail until man realises that he is one and that all life on your earth is connected. There are no 'sides', there are no 'enemies'. These are things of the ignorant mind. Differences of colour,

creed, race and religious belief – these are only physical differences. Underneath you are all parts of the same great spiritual family, there are no differences, no separations, this is what one has to realise. If you look at the macrocosm or the microcosm, whether you look at the global picture or whether you look at your own doorstep, the answer is the same – love your brother, love your neighbour, love yourself. Only in this way will the situation change.
Now, I know that you are eager to ask questions although I sense from you a little nervousness and trepidation, which is quite normal. Are you happy?"

Richard: "Yes".

White Feather: "Are *you* happy?"

Mandy: "Yes thank you"

White Feather: "Good. Thank you for giving me your voice. Don't be afraid. I don't bite; I am quite a normal chap really! If I can answer any questions that you put to me I will endeavour to do so. I always say that I am not a repository of all knowledge and wisdom. Like you I have a lot yet to learn and to unfold. That's as it should be, but if it falls within the orbit of my understanding and those who stand at my side, then I will do my best to answer it. I would add one final thing to that; I seek to win you over by reason. Don't accept anything that I say because I said it. If it does not concur with what lies within your heart then you must disregard it. I ask no 'faith' from you. What I impart to you does not require faith – this is not a religion. It requires only your reasoning mind and your questioning ability. You must discern what I say and decide whether you accept it or throw it out."

There followed several moments of silence, as if neither of the invited guests knew what to say to the spirit guide, before Richard gathered his thoughts together to ask the first question:

Richard: "You spoke of enlightenment. What do you mean by enlightenment?"

White Feather: "Enlightenment is the realisation of the divine within. By the divine I mean the Great Spirit, not an individual deity, not a God who sits upon some throne overlooking his creation — that is not God. The divine, the infinite, the eternal, the Great Spirit is everything that is — in your universe, the physical universe, in the spiritual universe, in your world and in my world, that is the Great Spirit. You are a part of that. The Great Spirit is within you, you are not separate from God in any way, but because you have much to learn, as do I, you are imperfect. You err, you stumble, you make mistakes, and this is natural. But where you can learn to go beyond your little self, beyond your personality, beyond your ego, beyond your attachment to the things you think are important and you learn to reside in the inner peace and wisdom of the eternal self, then you begin to attain enlightenment.

Enlightenment cannot be expressed in mere words because it is beyond the language of your earth. What you have to understand is that it is ultimate bliss and joy. It is eternal happiness. There are none in your world who have achieved true enlightenment. Some have come close to it. Some have glimpsed it as they would glimpse the sunrise in the morning and be encapsulated by its sheer simple beauty.

But it eludes them, because they still live in the world of form. When you can go beyond form to the formless, when you can go beyond matter and touch the divine, when your 'self' is lost and you become selfless and your thoughts are directed to others, to service, to altruism, to love, then you are touching upon enlightenment and that is the greatest state of all."

Sensing the atmosphere of nervousness that was developing, Amanda wisely sought to keep the energies flowing - an essential aspect of any sitting, by asking the next question:

Amanda: "White Feather, could you talk a little bit about the importance of meditation. Both the instrument through whom you speak and myself yesterday had an experience of meditation with a person who has had a big impact upon us. Can you talk a little about this?"

White Feather: "Yes I know of this, I was there don't forget! meditation is not an end in itself; it is a means to an end. There are many forms of meditation. As you know Sunflower you can meditate to music, you can enter into the silence or you can glimpse something beautiful – a sunrise, a flower, a butterfly, some simple yet profound words, the embrace of another – these are all forms of meditation for when you enter the meditative state you are entering an altered state of consciousness, you are leaving aside the world of form and matter and thought. You are going beyond thought into the realms of pure being. If you use a disciplined, well tried and tested method of meditation, that is acceptable, that is fine, there is no problem with that and meditation will always provide end results that are beneficial to you and to the soul.

Mediation can take many, many forms. Whatever suits you, whatever approach you take and feel comfortable with, is the right path for you. You will find that as you develop, so your meditation develops also. It will change, it will deepen. When you first begin, it is difficult, the mind is restless. It is like a fly that moves from here to there, it cannot be still, it cannot be settled and you think to yourself 'I cannot still my mind, I cannot empty my mind'. But the point is, to go beyond mind, beyond thought. This is difficult when you commence, but you will find that there will come a point when it suddenly becomes easy as if someone had switched a light on.

Do you remember Sunflower and you my friends – do you remember when you learned to swim? You can swim can't you? –and how difficult is was? You wouldn't let go of the side because you thought that you would sink? And now how easy it is! Remember when you learned to ride a bike? You perhaps don't remember learning to walk or to speak and you certainly don't remember learning to breathe – these things came automatically after a while. Breathing I assume came very quickly or you wouldn't be here! But you understand the point I am making – something that is difficult, somehow is transformed in to something simple, that you take as second nature. You take it for granted. Meditation is much like that, so whatever method you choose, if you feel comfortable with it, it is the right one and it will yield results."

Amanda: *"Do you still meditate in the spirit world?"*

White Feather: "Of course. Why give up something that is enjoyable? Just as you aspire to higher things, we do also."

Amanda: "What is it that you meditate for, given that last night we were sitting quietly in the silence and the teacher was talking about reaching a blissful stillness – is that what you aspire to still?"

White Feather: "Yes. You must not think that all life in the spirit realms is angelic, that we live in a constant state of bliss, because we don't. We still have our difficulties, we still have our imperfections, we still aspire to greater things – that is as it should be. It is an ongoing process and we still aspire to the same spiritual truths and the same Great Spirit as you do. You must understand that the knowledge that I impart for example does not always come from me – it comes through me. It is a waterfall. I obtain it from a higher source and pass it down to you. So I still have my work to do in these realms."

Noticing that the two visitors were still unusually quiet, the spirit visitor ventured to enquire if they had thought of another question yet:

Mandy: "They are all personal questions, not worldwide questions."

White Feather: "Ask. I can but try my best to answer."

At this point Mandy began sobbing, signifying an outpouring of emotional energy - a not infrequent response when someone encounters the love emitted by the guide and his helpers. White Feather, seeking to help, immediately responded with a question of his own:

"I hope those are tears of joy and not sadness?"

Mandy: "It's a very emotive question; why do I neglect myself?"

White Feather: "Let me look into your heart........yes. There is a part of you that doesn't like yourself in some way. There is no need for that, for you are a beautiful soul. Why do you punish yourself? Why do you tell yourself that you are not this, or not that, that you can't do this or can't do that? Yet you constantly prove yourself wrong. There is an inner battle, an inner conflict going on that is part of your growth, part of your development. You are too hard on yourself at times aren't you?"

Mandy: "Yes."

White Feather: "You don't need to be hard on yourself. You are not alone in present company. I can tell you that. You are not alone in present company - there are others here who are hard on themselves. It seems to be a human trait. It is fuelled I might add, by the culture in which you live, the society in which you live, where certain expectations are placed upon you, particularly on the female form but also on the male form where you are expected to conform to reach certain requirements and standards and are constantly made to feel inadequate or guilty. This is a worldwide phenomenon. If you could only see beyond this illusion, you would see my sister that you are a beautiful soul. Thinking now and talking not of the physical form, for that too has its beauty, I am speaking of the soul that lies within, that is beyond form, beyond matter, beyond the earth, beyond all the problems that you have. If you can touch that soul, if you can reach that inner centre – which you do at times when you open up your healing channel, then you will find that it is perfect in every way. It is beautiful and it is of the spirit.

The battles that you have, although they are at times, consuming for you and you think they are so important - in the fullness of time are not important. What is important is who and what you truly are as an individual. In that sense you are part of the Great Spirit. Allow that light to shine through you. Allow it to radiate through all the windows of your being and you will find that those problems that you seem to think are so important will melt away. Fact."

Turning to Amanda, the guide commented that she too fought her own personal gremlins:

"You understand what I am saying don't you Sunflower?" You also have battles don't you?"

Amanda: "Yes. I just want to do the right thing."

White Feather:"But what is the right thing? Is the right thing to give in to the wishes of another? Is the right thing to do what you know to be right within, even though at times it does not sit comfortably with others around you? It is a question here of being strong enough to adhere to what your inner self informs you. There is an inner guide – I call it the compass of the soul. It is always correct because it always points towards the truth, even though your conscious mind, your ego says 'no, you have to do this, you have to do that, you have to please this person, you have to please that person'. Underneath, if you listen, there is a voice that speaks to you as a still-small voice. It is the compass of the soul - it is the conscience. It knows more than you realise of what is true and if you follow that, even though it may be hard, you will find that it is always guiding you right."

Mandy: "Together Sunflower and I have had a very pleasant history doing Reiki and I am trying to develop my spiritual side but I feel that sometimes the forces of the human 3D world that we live in tends to take over my time and I don't feel that I have enough energy to incorporate that into my life as well and I feel that it is something that I really want to develop. How can I do that?"

White Feather: "It is a common problem regarding matters spiritual and in particular mediumship, in your world today. In times gone by mediums were able to devote more time to the development of their gifts because they did not have so many impositions in the world of matter. Today you have to compete with others, with relationships, with television, with your computers, with other devices that impose upon your time and energy as well as the many demands of your daily job and running a home. All of these things sap your energy. We realise this. You are not automatons. However any form of spiritual development requires discipline. If there is little discipline, there is little development. If you can put aside a little time on a regular basis, however short – perhaps fifteen or twenty of your minutes, then you will find that it will pay dividends. A little time spent harmonising with your soul and the energies of the spirit is better than none at all. It is the quality of that time and communication that is of the utmost, not the length of time that you open up. Do you understand that?"

Mandy: "Yes I do."

White Feather: "So if you can formulate – and I know that you can adhere to discipline because of the work that you undertake, if you can formulate a plan of action that gives a little time regularly, perhaps every day or every other day or so, then you will find that it will pay dividends. Not only will you be more comfortable in yourself, but you will find that your life becomes less burdensome and you can deal more easily with the various crises that arise from time to time because you are more connected to your higher self. Give it a try."

At this point, Richard, who had been sitting very quietly, listening to the wisdom being imparted by the sage, decided to ask a question that had obviously been troubling him deeply, opening his heart to all present and dramatically changing the direction of the gathering:

Richard: "Considering everything that you've spoken of, it might surprise you that if I were to say to you that due to the many, many terrible things that I've done in my lifetime I believe that I will be on this planet for a very long time as a form of punishment, what would you say to that?"

White Feather: "The Great Sprit does not punish. The Great Spirit does not stand over you when you pass into my world with a stick and say that you must be punished. What happens when you pass over, as you will do – as you all will, is that you will find a time of recollection where you will be able to consider in a measured way, your life upon the earth. You may find there are things that you realise that you wish you hadn't have done, whilst others, you wish that you had – this is a natural process. It can be little painful but no one will force you to come back upon the earth or subject you to any kind of punishment.

What however will happen is that your higher self will determine the next step – whether you continue your progress in my world or whether you reincarnate into another form upon the earth. Either way it won't be as a punishment, it will be as a way of allowing you to correct any imbalances, to work out any Karma and to continue your progress into the realms of light.

Even the lowest of the low son, those who are the most despotic minds – and you are far, far from that, are not condemned to eternal hell-fire, that doesn't exist. They have a price to pay and the price for sin is lack of progress but you are not condemned for all time, always there is a way to put right that which you believe you have done wrong and to rise again to the heights of understanding. So don't worry, don't beat yourself up too much. Does that hep you?"

Richard: "A little, yes."

White Feather: "Only a little?"

Mandy to Richard: "You have to let things go…."

Richard: "There are still answers there which I need."

White Feather: "Then ask. Ask more if you have something specific. I am looking into your heart now son and I know that you are……yes you are a good soul. You have made mistakes but then so have I, so have we all. You are imperfect, you are like many, many countless millions who have much yet to learn, but intrinsically you are not a bad soul."

Richard: "Thank you."

White Feather: "Ask your question."

Richard: "I......I err...."

As the visitor hesitated, stumbling over his response White Feather reassuringly pointed out that neither he nor anyone else from the next world was in a position to judge another:

White Feather: "Don't be afraid because I do not judge."

Richard: "Ok. I don't seem to be able to move on in my life at all because I don't think that what I did and how I handled things when my father died was right."

White Feather: "There is guilt there?"

Richard: "I don't know if you can call it guilt because guilt goes away and this doesn't."

White Feather: "Then you are still beating yourself up aren't you? You are still critical of yourself because of what you did or did not do?"

Richard: "Yes, because of what I did and didn't do. It wasn't right."

White Feather: "Do you think that your father is angry with you or critical of you? Because if you do then you are mistaken. I can tell you now there is no angst there; there is no anger, no bitterness, no no resentment. That is within you, not within the father who has passed, you have to understand that. I am being told this now. I do not have direct contact with that individual but I am being told this, that it is within your mind. Only you can let it go but there is no bitterness, no anger, no regret or hostility from this side of life. If nothing else that I say to you tonight makes any impact then let this do so because what I am saying to you is the absolute truth son."

Richard: "So if there is no bitterness from your side of where we are in this great scheme of things, then naturally you already know that there is bitterness on my side from family members."

White Feather:"Yes, but that is their concern, not yours. You cannot alter what others think or what they do – that is their pathway, that is *their* choice, *their* freewill. Happiness can only come from within yourself. If you are waiting for others to make you happy, then you will wait a long, long time. I can only say to that on a one to one level, from the one in my world to you, there is no problem. There is no cause for concern or bitterness or any other emotion of that kind. So what is stopping you being happy? If it is those around you upon the earth, then let them go their own way, let them have their tittle-tattle, let them have their disagreements, let them have their anger even if they direct it towards you. Find within yourself that contentment, that peace. There is nothing to stop that. Only you can stop that. If you want it you can have it but you have to let go of that feeling that you carry. Others can have their feelings but you do not need to take that on board son."

Continuing his debate with the guide, it seemed that nothing

White Feather said to reassure him that his father held no resentment eased his pain and Richard came back with another question that challenged the teacher's views on happiness:

Richard: "It's difficult because if we make ourselves happy, then why do we need others?"

White Feather: "Well, in the true essence of the question, you don't need others. That is the whole point. Many people believe that they need others to be happy – they need a girlfriend, they need a wife, they need a husband, they need a daughter, they need a son, they need parents, they need a car, a home, they need money, love – these things are transient. Happiness comes in knowing oneself and letting go of these things that matter. Let me say to you son – think of someone you love very much, if you can let that person go, then they will be with you always. When you try to hold them - that is when problems arise. A gardener has to learn to let go of a flower. If he holds it tight, he crushes it. This is what you have to do. Let go of all of those things that you think are so important, including others and you will find that so much will be added unto you. Think upon these words son. You may find a difficulty with them at first, but you will realise that what I am giving you is a wondrous opportunity. Take it, don't pass it up."

Becoming silent once more, as if to digest what the spirit councillor had said, the troubled guest conceded the floor once more to his fiancé, who sought to lighten the proceedings with a personal question of her own:

Mandy: "White Feather, the spiritual experiences that I have had, are they true of your world?

White Feather: "What do you mean by 'of my world'?"

Mandy: "Of the spiritual being - the higher world?"

White Feather: "The experiences that you have had are true to you, because you have had them. If you have endeavoured to work spiritually, then I can say to you that yes, what you have done is right. You have at times touched my world and others in my world have touched you and worked through you as they have done through Sunflower, particularly with the healing energies that you imbibe and that can only be a good thing. I think that the pathway that you are on is essentially the right one because within and beyond the material form there is a soul there that is of a good heart and desires to serve the spirit."

Mandy: "I totally understand what you say about how we are in this material world of wanting things and needing things to feel loved or to be somebody. One of the experiences that I had was when I felt that I visited the spirit world when everything thing that was around me wasn't with me if you understand and it really didn't matter. I totally understand what you are saying. The material things that I bought, the people that I was with, I didn't feel alone, I was ready to leave and I actually shouted out 'I am not scared…"

White Feather: "You find do you not, that when you are in that altered state you see things from a different perspective? Very often you know, when you are down in the valley you cannot see beyond the towering mountains that lie either side or ahead of you, but when you are transformed and stand upon the mountain top you can see to a new vista, a new horizon and things take on a far more grand appearance than they did when you were down in the depths. It is the same when you are able to leave the physical body – which you do each night by the way, when you sleep and at other times, through meditation or sometimes through a traumatic experience and you can see the material form with all its imperfections in a different light. You are not so held captive by it – you see it differently. This is what I think has happened to you from time to time."

Mandy: "Yes, although it hasn't happened for a while."

White Feather: "Well if it became commonplace then it would perhaps be too easy for you! It has to be a little difficult at times because then you strive, you look for spiritual experiences and you work towards them. When they do come they are all the more rewarding."

Mandy: "Am I choosing the right path with my career?"

White Feather: "Let me say that ultimately, your career will not bring you the fulfilment that you seek."

Mandy: "That is true. I know that already"

White Feather: "Yes, I know that from looking into your heart. It will not bring you fulfilment, it will only bring you temporary satisfaction and even that, is fleeting. There are other things for you. There are other avenues in life - there are other doorways that at the moment have been shut, that will open to you. When you reach those points in your life then they will open up, you won't have to knock. You will feel within yourself that it is time for a change. Already the seeds of that have begun to sprout within you and you feel that energy, that need, that desire for change. There is something holding you back to a point, which is natural because you have certain criteria that have to be fulfilled – monetary being one of them, but let me say to you that what lies deeply within will emerge and you will find that this impulse will grow stronger until you will be unable to resist it and you will make the change. Don't concern yourself yet, don't worry, there is a little water yet to go under the bridge before that time is reached, but I know that there are many adventures that lie ahead for you – many things, some to test you but many to fulfil you and enlighten you.

Never forget my sister that you are in essence a spirit with a body. You are not a body with a spirit. It is the spirit that is the real you and when you begin to allow the spirit to shine and light to radiate through all the portals of your being, then you will touch many souls upon life's journey and that will bring you fulfilment that is beyond words."

Spirit guides such as White Feather are often sensitive to the thoughts of sitters, recognising a question that may be forming in their mind even before it is spoken aloud. Knowing that Richard was formulating just such a question, the sage spoke first, speculating what the nature of the enquiry might be:

"I feel another question coming here and I think it is a big one!"

Richard: "You spoke of others standing with you. Who is standing with you?"

White Feather: "Well I can't tell you everyone because I will say to you – and this will surprise you, that there are over a thousand here this night. Some who work within the direct group relating to the medium and to Sunflower, some who operate within your immediate soul group and many who come because they wish to take part in the proceedings and also observe. As I speak to this gathering I am speaking also to many in my world who can listen, watch, observe and partake in the proceedings. So not only are you being helped, they are being helped also and it is a wondrous thing."

Richard: "Another question – please don't take this the wrong way, it may sound rather negative, but from some of the things you have said this evening, particularly the conversation about the gardener who holds onto the flower too tightly and crushes it, are you actually saying that if I let go of my family, my partner, my job, that I will actually be happy?"

White Feather: "Not in the sense that you turn your back on them all and expect everything to fall into place. I am not suggesting that at all, because of course you have to obtain the coin of your world, you have to feed yourself, you have to pay your bills and it would be irresponsible to let go of the requirements that you need to survive upon the earth. What I am saying to you is - let go emotionally of the ties. If you can learn to let go of the importance, the attachment to them, then you will find that you are indeed letting go of something very important. You will enter into a state where the very thing that you are letting go of, will be drawn to you. The Nazarene, or Jesus as you may know of him, once said to his disciples 'let go of all your possessions, sell all your worldly possessions and follow me'. What was it that he meant by that? It was an analogy for the same spiritual truth that I am seeking to impart to you – by letting go of something you are actually holding onto it, it is almost an opposite in operation, but it is a supreme truth. It is when you become so attached to a material form and value it and hold it so tightly, that it actually traps you. When you learn to let it go, inwardly in your thoughts, then it remains with you. Do you understand what I am saying?"

Richard: "I think so, yes. Because I wouldn't let go of my father, my family or my job or any of that. You spoke of survival and survival is important."

Sensing that Richard had not quite grasped his point about non-attachment, despite his affirmative reply, White Feather continued to press home his response:

White Feather: "But you see, by 'letting go' of your partner I am not suggesting that you push them away. If there is a link of love there, then you have no need to hold them. If you set them free, will they not remain with you, because they love you? If they did not love you then they would not remain with you. Then why would you hold them anyway? That would not be real love. The real values, the real things if they are meant to be, will remain. Ultimately, if we take this to its conclusion, if you were to trust in the power of the spirit to serve you, then you would indeed set yourself free from your material labour because the law would operate in such a way that you would find that things were made available to you. You would not starve, you would not lose everything, something would come your way. The problem is that somewhere deep inside you don't really believe that and that intent changes the dynamics of the situation."

Richard: *"That's true."*

To yet further emphasise the validity of his teaching, the spirit visitor delivered a suitable analogy to try and win over his earthly visitor, whose stubbornness had become a block to his own progress:

White Feather: "So many people in this world have that. You've seen people son haven't you, walk across hot coals. Why don't they get burned? Because they have the belief that they won't. If somewhere in that belief there is a little doubt that creeps in because they don't really believe it, then they get burned. That is the difference. That is what I am speaking of here. Let go and you will find that you will be given so much in that letting go. There is no loss without gain, there is no giving without receiving. As you let go, so you draw so much more in its place."

Richard: *"Unfortunately I find there is no gain without loss. For what I gave, I must lose."*

White Feather: "That is your opinion."

Richard: *"Very often it is true."*

White Feather:"Think deeply upon what I have said son. Think beyond the surface of it. Think into it, because we are speaking here of spirit laws that are very profound. They operate regardless of your belief, regardless of my belief. The truth is the truth is the truth. Whatever you or I believe it doesn't alter the way that the law operates."

Mandy: *"On that note, I've chosen Richard as my life partner, I am a very positive person as you may have experienced and Richard is quite negative, how can we infuse the two and bring us together into the same – singing the same song. I desire this so much but I feel I am banging my head against a wall, trying to make him understand that the glass is half full as opposed to half empty?"*

White Feather: "There are always two ways of looking at things as you realise and although the spirit laws operate in such a way that like attracts like, very often you find that in relationships, opposites also attract and sometimes this can work in that the one will balance the other or offset the other and at times, over certain periods it can have an adverse effect – it can cause disharmony and discord. What I would say to you ultimately is that where there is true love, real love, then all obstacles will be surmounted and nothing will keep you apart. Many people – and I am speaking now in a broader context, believe that they are in love when they are not. They think that they have found their soul mate or their life partner when in reality, they haven't. Where there is true love, there is no discord, there is no disharmony, it is only surface. Yes, you may have your disagreements, you may argue from time to time but underneath, underpinning that, there is a deeper love and respect and a realisation that one has found one's other half. You have to realise that where there is true love, there can be no discord. So it is self-fulfilling, it will always come right. Whatever disharmony arises between you, if you truly love each other then always you will find that you are drawn back together magnetically. Nothing will keep you apart, not even death. Do you understand that?"

Mandy: *"Totally, yes. Is there anything upon our pathway that we are allowed to know?"*

White Feather: "Well it wouldn't be kind of me to disclose all of life's secrets. There are reasons why you do not have full access to your pathway and all of the many adventures that lie upon it. There are reasons why, because some of the things that you pass through are karmic – you have to outwork them, and others are as a result of your ongoing freewill which determines certain course and life changes along the pathway. There are reasons why you don't know the answers to everything and you don't know all the things that are going to occur because if you did, then some of you would seek to avoid them and that would not be beneficial.

You have to know darkness to know light, you have to sometimes be captive to know freedom and you have to come through ignorance to find truth. Rest assured that whatever lies upon your pathway you will emerge through it. You will come unscathed from it because the spirit that is the real you, is indestructible. Things of matter will come and go – they are transient. They will rust, they will tarnish, they will decay, but the things of the spirit, the higher aspects of the soul, the qualities that you each have, the character that you have developed, the ability to love and to serve others and to help, to be kind and to be gentle - these things endure into eternity. All is known."

Mandy: *"Does that include my family as well?"*

White Feather: "If you are expecting me, my sister, to say that you will all have a life free from pain and suffering, I cannot. But ultimately you are all eternal because you are of the Great Spirit. You cannot die, not one of you can die. You cannot die for the life of you! So don't worry. You are all worriers. You worry about this, you worry about that! You worry about what might happen tomorrow, you worry about what happened yesterday – all this worry consumes you and uses your energy. Let it go, don't let it disturb the tranquillity of your being. Hold on to that inner sense of happiness and joy and the very fact that you are infinite and eternal. What greater truth and knowledge can you have than this?"

With her partner once again in silent contemplation of his next question, Mandy continued to seek answers of a more spiritual nature:

Mandy: "Do the angels work alongside us?"

White Feather: "Angels come in many forms. They don't have wings. You may think they do, but they don't. There are angels in my world, there are angels in your world. They take many forms. They work at your side, they work to help humanity, to help suffering souls upon your earth and in my world in the lower planes. You yourself may be an angel to another, remember that. Angels don't always come on clouds with harps and wearing white robes! They can appear in the strangest guises. All that matters is that they serve. Service is the coin of the spirit. As you are served, so you should serve others. In service there is the greatest joy and in service you are helped because your own soul quickens and you are able to reach a higher degree of unfoldment and spiritual awareness."

Opening his heart once more, Richard took the opportunity to reveal his innermost feelings about himself, particularly concerning his perceived behaviour around the time of his father's passing as the sitting once again took a dramatic turn. White Feather though, was steadfast in his response:

Richard: "White Feather, Mandy believes that if a certain thing happens or she gets a certain feeling, she goes and seeks advice from her angel cards and they give answers, whereas I'm just the opposite – I am very much a believer that there is no fate but what we make ourselves, thus again, backtracking slightly, I was a complete 'git' to my father, so he was taken away from me."

White Feather: "It doesn't work like that son and you know it. You know it deep inside. That is only a part of you punishing yourself. We have already gone through this and if you read through the transcript of this tape you will know that what I said to you earlier still applies. You have yet to let that go. Regarding the cards, they are but one form of focus for the mind. There are many ways that the mind or the consciousness can focus to attain a changed state in order to access information. It is not the cards that reveal the truth but the focused mind that taps in to a different dimension, that uncovers it, whether you use cards, crystal balls, divining or any other physical means it is still the spiritual and mental aspects that yield the results."

Mandy: "Is it my interpretation of what those cards mean that gives me the answers that I desire?"

White Feather: "That is an aspect of it, but more so it is your ability to tune in to the energies and the fields that lie beyond the material consciousness."

Amanda: "We've had this conversation because I've used cards as a way of training my mind and disciplining it to look beyond. I can work the other way but as White Feather said, it isn't intrinsically what the card is, it is the fact that you've used that as a portal for the greater knowledge that is there and that you can access. I feel that sometimes we need to have a little bit of help."

Mandy: "Yes, that's why I only use them when I feel the need to use them, not every day or every week. I feel that's my connection to the spiritual world."

White Feather: "That is so, but you could also make the connection when you are ready, without the cards. That is the next step. It is not so far away, it is closer than you think."

Richard: "I understand that, but from some of the things you've said this evening White Feather, there is a good and a bad balance in everything. Now, from a deck of angel cards there is no negative, there is no bad, so how can that be realistic if there is good and bad in everything?"

White Feather: "Everything has its balance as you say. Good and bad, high and low, negative and positive, male and female – sometimes that which you consider to be bad is good and sometimes what man considers to be good, is bad, because you look from one perspective.

Sometimes you can see things from one angle whereas we see them differently. Ultimately the truth lies within. It doesn't lie in cards. It doesn't lie in the book or the temple. It doesn't lie in the great orator – it lies within your own heart and you can come into truth without any of these props because you sense it, you are in alignment with it, you are in harmony with it. I often say to people that truth lies beyond words -you can just know something. They say to me 'how can you just know something?' I say to them that it is because they are in alignment with it, they are in attunement with it. Truth does not require language. It does not require any trappings – the truth is. It always has been and it always will be. It is the same today as it was yesterday. You only have to put yourself in harmony with it and you absolutely know that you are right."

As the evening began to reach its conclusion, Mandy made one final attempt to find a way of resolving her partner's inner turmoil by asking the guide if there was anything further she could do to ease his pain:

Mandy: "What can he [Richard} and I do to help Richard let go of this grief that he is still holding onto so tightly with his family?"

White Feather: "You have to ask yourself what you are getting from it - what good is it giving you? What happiness is it bringing you? Do you feel comfort from beating yourself up and feeling guilty? If you find the key to this – which is what you are getting from it, then you will find the answer to your problem. The answer, as I have already said to you is not complex, it is simple – let go of that which you no longer need. It is your lower mind which is holding that. Your soul doesn't want it. Your father doesn't want it and ultimately you don't want it, so let it go. I cannot put it any other way. I am not going to dress it up for you. It is as simple as that.

You walk one step in front of another don't you? You don't have to take a big leap here, only a little step. Always remember that – only a little step. That little step is the biggest leap you will ever make."

It had been an evening of many twists and turns with the emotionally charged atmosphere bringing the best out of the guide as he compassionately yet uncompromisingly tried to resolve the sitters' difficulties. As the group said their farewells to the sage, he could not help but deliver one final message:

White Feather: "Sunflower, we will have to take our leave now as we are drawing close to the time of vacation. Is there anything else that you would ask of me before I depart?"

Mandy: "Thank you for coming and visiting us and allowing us to speak to you. I do appreciate it and send you great love."

Richard: "Thank you so much for your guidance and help and certainly I will try an apply what you have said."

White Feather: "Son, don't try……'

Mandy & White Feather spontaneously: "…….Do!"

Following the withdrawal of the spirit control and the return to

normality by the medium, a conversation ensued between everyone present in which Richard outlined in greater detail the difficulties that he endured as a result of what he described as his treatment of his father at the time of his passing to the spirit world. Whether or not the guide had been able to reach within his heart to turn him around, remains to be seen. Guilt can be a very heavy burden to carry and often it can only be released when the deeper understanding attained through spiritual development is applied. Even White Feathers' reassurance that Richard's departed father held no grudge against him, appeared not enough to change his view.

Ultimately change must come from within, but one thing is certain - the seeds that were sown by our friend from the next world will one day germinate, for as the guide himself has been known to utter 'nothing is ever lost'.

"What we do unto others, we do to ourselves"

Eight
Animal instincts

White Feather has always spoken with great affection about the animal kingdom. Knowing how many of those who follow his teachings are also animal lovers, a meeting was arranged to enable a small, dedicated group to put their questions to him concerning the animal kingdom. When the meeting had to be postponed due to circumstances beyond our control it was decided that the group should email their questions and Amanda would then put them before the guide, combining them with some of her own. The resulting session produced some interesting answers, starting with one concerning the philosophy of Buddhism, which produced a concise reply:

Amanda: "I have an interest in the Buddhist philosophy and I want to ask you this question; from what you have told us, a human would not be able to reincarnate as an animal because the human spirit has evolved beyond it. Is that correct?"

White Feather: "The lesser cannot contain the greater."

Amanda: "Yes, I see that but I don't understand where their thoughts come from. Would you be able to elaborate upon that – on where the Buddhist way of thinking concerning the concept of reincarnating back into a lower animal form originates?"

White Feather: "Whether the original source gave that teaching in a metaphorical sense and it has since been misconstrued, I am not certain – that is certainly a possibility, just as the many teachings given in the Biblical sense have also been misconstrued -the teaching of the Nazarene, either taken literally or else twisted. This is a fault in mans' psyche. I can only speak with what I know to be fact and once having attained the human condition, there is no going back to what is effectively a lower vibration. Even though animals can exhibit wonderful traits – loving traits, spiritual traits, they do not possess the same level of development spiritually as man does."

Amanda: "So would it not be true that if you create Karma in the human physical existence than you have to repay that Karma in the same way that you created it?"

White Feather: "Yes. If you create karma in a certain place and time then you have to return to that place, although not necessarily that time, to readdress that karma, to rebalance, to re-harmonise. It is no good thinking that you can create a problem in one place and solve it in another. Although some aspects can be outworked in the spirit realms, more often than not you have to return to the source, the scene where one created a disturbance in order to correct it."

Armed with the list of questions received in advance of the

sitting, Amanda read out the first of several well crafted enquiries, a question which the guide had been asked before, knowing that the sage would respond as always, without a moments hesitation:

Amanda: *"Is the soul purpose of animals to help the human evolve or are they on their own journey? Or, are they only here to support our planet? What is their true purpose?"*

White Feather: "You have to understand that life has evolved upon the earth as it has throughout the boundless universe and many other worlds such as yours. The purpose of that evolution is to assist and enable the spirit to gain ever-greater expression. Without the animal kingdom there would not be the human kingdom because there would not have been the necessary amount of evolution having taken place to enable the human condition to come into being. So you have to have this progression from the lower to the higher, from the simple to the complex. Spirit comes through the animal kingdom as it comes through preceding forms of life – the bird, the fish, the insect, the vegetable, the mineral, the sub-atomic form. Spirit comes through all of these levels which assist its entry into your world and eventually, over the course of evolution, the higher more complex, more refined vehicle is created or emerges from the evolutionary track and allows the higher expression of spirit to function through it. In the case of your earth, this is termed the human form. So animals play their part in assisting that progress and procession to take place."

Q: *"I have read your wise words in three wonderful books where you say that the human evolves from the tiniest insect upwards. This indicates from where we progress our consciousness. If this is correct, does it follow that we are debilitating the evolution of our consciousness, which I understand is the soul essence, when we hurt and destroy both our animal and plant life?"*

White Feather: "The simple answer to that is yes. Anyone – any individual or group who denigrate any form of life, whether it is a fellow human, animal, bird, fish or insect, particularly where they act out of knowledge, denigrates their own progress. What is done to others is done to the self. What you give out, you receive. What you sow, you reap. At the moment man is inflicting great suffering upon the animal kingdom for various reasons – for the food chain, for scientific research, or out of pure spite and evil. All actions reflect upon those who carry out those actions. So if you give out negative actions, if you are hurtful, then you are reflecting that same energy back to yourself. You are drawing it back to yourself."

The next question was asked on behalf of a lady who works tirelessly to rescue and care for injured birds and whose sanctuary is home to many feathered friends whose lives she and her husband have helped to save:

Q: *"Is it truthful to say that humans interfere with nature on a destructive scale? For example; there is a trend to capture and transport wild animals around the world for the commercial pet trade. The very few who survive this ordeal are then kept in small receptacles or enclosures. In order to defer the wild, intrinsic nature of the animal, the human facilitates generations of manageable and amenable immature animals from human companionship by stealing away eggs* and offspring from their natural parents for artificial incubation and hand rearing. These actions cause immeasurable physical, emotional and psychological suffering. Whether for commercial or other means is there any rhyme or reason, or justification for what I consider a merciless crime against nature?"

White Feather: "I can see none. Man is grossly ignorant in his lack of understanding and his treatment, not only of his fellow man but of the animal kingdom in particular. He will always find reasons for his actions. He will always find excuses for his behaviour, but unless he strives to act from his higher self, from his spiritual soul level of understanding, then I do not see any change in these practices. It is to the detriment of his spiritual progress that he continues upon this pathway in my view."

Q: "What is the consensus of parrots' feelings about being in captivity?"

White Feather: "I don't think, from what I call tell of linking with the animal kingdom, that any creature in the truest sense likes to be captive. At whatever level, the true essence of spirituality is freedom. You cannot imprison the soul so why should you try to imprison the physical form? The true essence of spirit is to be flowing, to be free, to be able to spread its wings — metaphorically and in many cases, literally. So it is not natural to confine any creature, even though I know sometimes it is done for the right reasons — to protect the species. Sometimes even the captor and the captive share an affinity and love, for even the prisoner can love his gaoler. But the simple answer is that all forms were created and evolved to be free in their natural habitat and that I think, should be encouraged wherever possible."

Picking up on the guide's reply, Amanda asked the teacher a question of her own concerning a deeper reason for keeping animals captive:

Amanda: "Just following on from that, if there are birds that are rescued from sometimes a fate worse than death, is there then a reason for them being in captivity? Is the reason to offer them a much better life than they would have had?"

White Feather: "Yes, because the motive is to save the species. Man is making extinct on a daily basis so many creatures and forms upon your earth that naturally there are those who through their awareness and their spirituality, through their love for creation, are trying to offset this, to prevent it and to restore balance and harmony. They act from their highest principles in trying to save the species, even by making it captive. It is the motive that counts."

Q: "Also, in those animals that are used in scientific experiments, do they feel that their sacrifice is worth it or do they simply suffer the pain and are not aware of the purpose of the experiment?"

White Feather: "On an individual level the animal does suffer pain and is not aware of the reasons, but the soul group of that species is compensated. No animal ever suffers without there is compensation. The compensation to the group soul of that species is that it is quickened through the suffering of the many forms that make up that collective."

Q: "So, can the human really cure his or her physical suffering from the pain and suffering that laboratory experiments cause to millions of animals throughout the world every year? If so, does this affect the evolution of that person's soul?"

White Feather: "It does affect the evolution of the individual and man as a collective, as a whole. There is an old saying; 'two wrongs don't make a right'. You may obtain some temporary satisfaction and temporary cure through experimentation upon defenceless creatures but ultimately this disquiet, this disharmony will manifest in some other way because the law operates with perfection and you cannot through inflicting suffering and pain upon anyone, expect to create harmony and peace and happiness. What you sow, you reap. What man sows, he reaps and if man sows seeds of suffering then he will reap suffering."

Amanda: "I have a question that in one way concerns animals. If you are going to eat in the spirit world, can you choose to do that by thought alone? If you really enjoy your meal upon the earth plane, can you continue to do that and can you physically eat?"

White Feather: "You can have the equivalent of what you would call food. If I want to eat a vegetable, then I can have that vegetable, if I want to take a drink then I can consume that drink but I do not have the physical organs to digest it as you do. Neither would I need to excrete waste or take energy from what I consume in that manner. The realisation quickly dawns on the people in my world that energy is obtained from the very ether in which they exist. The very level upon which they find themselves, feeds them and gives them energy and vitality. They do not need to obtain it through the old habits — that is what they are. A residue of habitual behaviour can still remain after death but there is no need to consume food."

Amanda: "So in that respect, talking about animals, I personally choose not to eat meat because I don't like the thought of doing that knowing the suffering that animals have to go through, but if you have someone who has been a big meat eater whilst on earth, surely it is their own mind that creates this illusion that they have to kill meat and consume it?"

White Feather: "Yes. It perpetuates and it continues. Where there are well-entrenched and developed patterns of behaviour and where the mind has been conditioned to being expected to participate in certain activities and ways of behaving, these can persist after death and it can take a little time for realisation to dawn that it is no longer necessary to perpetuate these beliefs."

Q: "Would most pets prefer to be with humans or would they prefer the companionship of their own species? Is this concept of 'companion animals' simply a human concept of companionship?"

White Feather: "Not entirely. As I said earlier it is my understanding and belief that in the true sense, the spirit should be free and all animals should be able to live freely in their correct environment — the environment into which they have evolved. Having said that, the relationship between human and animal, if it is a loving one, is a wonderful thing and the animal or creature, if it has reached that level of spiritual and mental development will respond to the love and companionship of the one termed its 'owner'. Sometimes, I think it is the pet that owns its master!

So here you are seeing a higher spiritual principle at work. You are seeing a higher trait emerge — the relationship between the so-called owner, who is supposed to be more intelligent and its pet and this is a wonderful thing to behold. There is a deeper aspect to this because where this relationship develops then the energy of the creature, the soul essence is quickened and it is helped along its own pathway of evolution. You know, as I have said before that the spirit that animates creatures will one day come through a higher form, most notably human."

Amanda: "It's funny that you should say that because we've noticed recently that our cat and rabbit — the rabbit particularly, have developed their own character and we almost feel that they own us. The rabbit has a decision making process......"

White Feather: "I've no doubt about that!"

Amanda: "It makes us feel guilty though, the fact that we've no right to 'own' pets, but having said that our motive is a sound one because if we were to let the rabbit go he would not survive."

White Feather: "So your motive is a good one. In reality Sunflower, you don't own him. You own nothing. You don't even own the clothes that you wear. The fact that you can give him love, that you can share your understanding and spirituality with such a creature and do so in such a kind way can only benefit you both because even though you feel a little guilt that you imprison that creature in his home, you do your best to let him out and give him a sense of freedom and you do that because your motive is to help him and to protect him. It is the motive that counts."

A question that so often concerns animal lovers is whether or not their beloved pet will be with them in the next life and if they will progress together in the spirit realms. This topic was addressed by White Feather when he once again reiterated the power of love:

Q: "After a companion animal has been re-united with his guardian (in the spirit world) will the former progress and move on with the latter or will the animal have to be left behind and ultimately return to the group soul of its species? Is it also possible for the animal soul to reincarnate into the devic or elemental kingdom?"

White Feather: "If I can take the latter aspect first – the devic kingdom, the elemental kingdom is on a different evolutionary path than the animal kingdom. The animal does not transmigrate, just as the human soul does not go back into the animal form so the animal does not transmigrate into the devic form. It has to progress after death and if there is a love between the creature and its former owner upon the earth then they can continue to progress together through the planes of my world but I must say that ultimately it is not the destiny of the animal to continue indefinitely. You have to realise that the spirit that works through that creature has to express through a higher form and come into the human condition, so there will be a point where the animal form will be surrendered and the spirit that has worked through it will come again into a human form."

Amanda: *"Could you just explain a little further about devas and what they are?"*

White Feather: "There are many life streams – human is one, there are many species that come under the auspices of the animal kingdom, there are other forms, what you would refer to as the devic kingdom and nature spirits that do not incarnate into physical form. Their work is to assist nature, to assist the mineral, vegetable and animal kingdoms in their journey upon the earth. Just as you have helpers, guides and friends that assist you – because no one is ever alone upon the earth, so the animal kingdom, the plant kingdom and the mineral kingdom too have their helpers, guides and guardians. These come under many labels because again it is the old problem of semantics, but essentially these streams of consciousness do not touch the earth, they do not have the need for a physical evolution. Their work is from the etheric and astral realms to help the lower forms of life in their expression upon the earth."

Q: *"It has been said that the creation of so-called pests such as fleas, lice, bugs etc. is due to base, evil thoughts of humans. If this is the case, what happens to the above once they pass over? Do they become part of the group-pool and eventually progress too?"*

White Feather: "Well it is not so, because there were such creatures upon your earth long before man evolved. There were all kinds of insect forms upon the earth as part of the evolution of life – long before man evolved. So I do not concur with the view that they are as a result of mans' thinking. You have to realise that what appears as a pest to you or I, in the greater scheme of things is not so. Everything exists because it has a purpose. The flea has a purpose, the fly has a purpose, the snake has a purpose, the spider has a purpose. Even though you may abhor these creatures, they each play a part in helping to create and maintain a balance within nature. The fly for example – its role is to help decompose matter, to return excrement to its natural state and help break it down. Now you may say, 'what is the purpose of an insect that carries a virus from human to human or from animal to human?' but again, you see that it all comes within the overall scheme and balance of life. Life is not meant to be permanent upon the earth. Life comes and goes – it lives and it dies in the physical sense. Every insect and every form is there for a purpose – there is no abomination in God's kingdom."

It had been another intriguing sitting, with a diverse range of questions put to the guide, some of which to our knowledge, he had not been asked before. That he is always able to deliver such immediate, thought provoking replies is a testament to his spiritual understanding and wisdom. Some may not agree with all of his answers, whilst in others they may provoke yet more questions, but this is the beauty of communicating with the spirit sage. For through this dialogue we can stretch our minds whilst at the same time expand our understanding of matters which are often overlooked or taken for granted. The issue surrounding captive wild animals is complex with far-reaching implications for the individual animal. The motive behind the

the action to save a wild species in captivity, whether good or bad, still causes the animals to suffer on various levels. Captivity inhibits freedom of expression and so it is to the detriment of the wild essence within the individual animal. This is a crime against nature and the natural law and White Feather and others of his ilk go to great lengths to remind us of this fact. We ignore their warnings at our peril.

"You cannot cage the spirit. You cannot imprison the soul"

Nine
A glimpse of the future

"As I join with you tonight there is a recognition of the purpose that unites us, for we seek to serve the same divine power that seeks to reveal itself and all its boundless wonder to those who search for truth and understanding. I link with you this night in response to the thoughts that you hold paramount in your mind and also because of the affinity that I share with that which lies innermost, in the very sanctuary of your being.
I know that deep within your heart you care for the future of mankind and for all those children of the Great Spirit who are engaged actively upon the same pathway of unfoldment."

With those words White Feather began his talk one evening as as he took control of his instrument in order to deliver his address. The request had been 'sent out' asking if he would say a few words about the future of mankind to help the many people struggling for survival upon this earth, whose lives are blighted by fear and ignorance. Indeed, it seems that the world in which we live is one in which more and more restrictions are

being imposed upon us in the name of 'democracy'. Some would argue that these violations of basic freedom are necessary to maintain law and order in violent times, whilst others would argue with some justification that true freedom comes not through the erosion of civil liberties and human rights but through proper education and the understanding and implementation of true spiritual laws.
White Feather it would seem, is aware of the undercurrents that are driving the world towards a global totalitarian state. His words do not make easy reading, as he predicts dark times ahead for mankind. Yet as always, his knowledge and trust in the higher spiritual laws reveal an eventual outcome that is more positive and his optimism that the truth and light will prevail give us all hope and encouragement for the future:

"You have asked me to comment upon the future, as a way of giving direction to those who read the words contained within this volume. Yet requesting this of me presents me with a difficulty, for it is like asking me to count the leaves upon a tree or the number of reflections of sunlight glistening upon an ocean, or even the grains of sand upon a beach. For the future is boundless. It is infinite. When you ask 'what does the future hold for mankind?' of which point in the future do you speak? If you are talking about mankind's future as a race then its ultimate destiny is one of joy, of fulfilment. Because man is of the Great Spirit and the Great Spirit is all encompassing love and truth, then man collectively and individually must also embrace those same qualities. As I've said to you many times, perfection is achieved only in eternity and I cannot select a point in time when each and every aspect of the divine has attained self-realisation. I do know however, that man can hinder and in some limited ways thwart his progress, although ultimately he cannot prevent it and it is perhaps the future that lies closest to you at this point in time which concerns me most. For many who are aware of these words that I am now speaking will also be aware of feelings of disquiet, discomfort and uncertainty within themselves. This is as a result largely, of mans' own actions and the changes that he imposing upon society and every individual contained within it. For man is very much concerned with the material form, with substance – the tangible world, the physical expression that absorbs so much of his thinking and deeds. Yet as I have said many times this is an illusionary world. It is a misnomer in many senses because although it presents that facet of the soul that is incarnate in matter with the opportunity to experience upon many levels, it also presents many obstacles and many illusions that have to be overcome and transcended.

In this level in which you currently reside, the ego has its play and you will find that in many walks of life and in many aspects it is the egos of men driving forward, often to the detriment of their higher spiritual selves. The ego aligns itself with identity, with form, with substance, with that which empowers it and gives it a sense of self-importance. But often, it will engineer and bring about circumstances, events and experiences that strengthen its own position, which is one of *perceived* power. In reality it has little power except that which it imagines. Even so, it is strong and at times powerful and is a master manipulator of circumstances. But what the discerning mind has to understand and realise is that the ego *is not the great master that it appears.*"

The teacher went on to reveal more about the nature of the human ego and the many ways in which it seeks to 'fool' the

mind into succumbing to its wishes by any devious means at its disposal:

"You have to see through its guises, which are many and varied. You have to recognise it for what it is particularly when it applies to your own decision making, for the ways in which you conduct your lives and the morals and standards that you live by. Of course there are those in your world who recognise the various traits of the ego and play to them. They write scripts that can be delivered unto the role-playing aspect of the individual who diligently and duly carries them out as if like an actor in a play upon the stage of life. And so, you get those who assume self-importance and grandeur, who wield temporary control over others to gather around them like minds who feed their ego state. So this myth, this illusion is perpetuated and circumstances and events arise upon your world, often with dire consequences which are crafted to fulfil a certain agenda. At the moment you have the unfolding of a pathway that is taking mankind collectively into a situation that will ultimately be detrimental to the higher soul state. Artificial events are being manipulated into being and circumstances are being created to establish a climate of suspicion, of fear, of trepidation, of anguish and of suffering. For political and state purposes the few are manipulating the many. Solutions to man-made problems are being offered as the electronic age of surveillance and manipulation of every soul upon the planet is ushered into being. You are told that the state is your protector, that the state cares for you, the state loves you, that you should be proud to be a citizen and patriotic to the cause. But these illusions fool many into accepting the erosion of their liberties and what should be their true free state of thought.

Continuing his talk, the guide revealed how those seeking to control world events through manipulating 'reality' often stage-manage events such as wars in order to create confusion and fear because they know that a fearful mind is more easily suggestible, but explains that ultimately the soul cannot be held captive:

"You cannot cage the spirit. You cannot imprison the soul and yet in many ways, this is what some are trying to establish in your world as they tighten their grip and their control through various means. Brother is set upon brother. Wars are created. Lives are lost in the physical sense. The landscape is obliterated. The beauty and harmony that should prevail in your world is replaced by pain, suffering and darkness. The light of truth is obscured by the clouds of ignorance. You are offered 'solutions' that create only more problems. You are offered answers that only produce more questions and until mankind as a whole begins to turn inward to the subtle planes wherein lie truth and understanding, love, harmony, light and oneness, will this state of affairs change.

You have to realise that you bring into being the reality that you see and sense around you. Those who are your manipulators and would be captors recognise that if they feed and stimulate the senses of man in a certain way, then they can achieve certain results. The wise soul sees through the illusion. The wise soul recognises the illusion for what it is because it can see the greater reality that lies behind it. It is a fool who follows fools. It is a wise man that follows his heart. Within you lie the answers to all things. The immediate future of your world and of mankind is difficult. I wish I could paint you a rosy picture of a century that stretches out before you, bringing increased harmony, co-operation and love between individuals and nations, but from where I view the opposite is true. There will be wars, there will be darkness, there will be confusion, there will be fragmentation upon many levels as the ignorant have their day. But I want you all to recognise that in these times of difficulty the divine light of the spirit which has created and continues to create the boundless universe with its myriad of forms, which keeps the stars and planets in their orbits, which brings life and light to the darkest corners, is aware of this situation and is watching over events. As I have said, man can hinder and delay, but he cannot prevent the plan of the Great Spirit from outworking itself. Man thinks he has great power, but he has little power in true terms. Compared to the real power of the spirit, of the divine intelligence that created everything that is, mans' power is very, very limited.

I have said sometimes in the past that it is darkest just before the dawn. You are entering into that time. There will be periods of great darkness when you will be fearful, when you will be filled with despair and hopelessness, but I say these things not to frighten you, but to let you know that in the midst of this turmoil will come peace, will come light and will come truth. This will not come in the form of a saviour God or any individual sent to your earth to create miracles. It will come through enlightenment of man as a race. Even now change has begun. Even as I speak there are many who are turning inward, who are questioning, who are searching and looking deeper within, beyond their material form and its limitations. They are finding and recognising the divine and the infinite that lies within them. This is a sea change. It is a change of enormous proportions. Energies will come to mankind that will enable this transformation of consciousness to take place, but it won't be overnight. It won't be in a day or a week or a year. It will be over generations of time. Slowly and surely the darkness will be replaced by light. The sun will rise and shine again and man, captivated and controlled through his own ego state, will be released and will set himself free as the divine power of the spirit is realised within.

So when you ask me to speak of the future, these are my words to you. What I am offering you is a double-edged sword. One the one hand you have the unfolding of events that have already begun, on the other you have the deeper, more profound spiritual change that also has begun."

Reiterating that ultimately the higher purpose of God will triumph over the darkness of ignorance, the guide, whose words have helped many a weary soul across the years of his communications with this world concludes his talk, firstly with a wonderful analogy and finally with a heartfelt plea to us all to always remember the divinity that lies within:

"When you look at an ocean that is stormy, where the seas rise, the winds blow and the waves crash, you cannot always see the deep residing peace that lies beneath the surface. When the hurricane batters the coast, the trees are bent backwards and the leaves shake and tremble you cannot always see the roots that go deep into the ground. You have to look with the eyes of the spirit. The all-loving God that is your creator, of which you are always a part, will never desert you. Truth will win through the day because it has to. Truth is stronger than ignorance, light is stronger than darkness, hope is greater than despair – do not forget these things. Align yourself always with the highest and best that you can and remember the awesome power that resides within and around you.

I hope these words find a lodgement within your heart. I hope that you remember them in times of difficulty because they are given from one who can glimpse what lies ahead. It is one thing to have faith but it is another to know the truth. When the storms of life hit you, sometimes faith is not enough, but if you have truth then you have built your house of understanding upon solid ground. So seek truth and add faith unto it and you will find through this that you will achieve a steadfastness that is formidable and enable you to withstand any storm of life that comes your way.

Recognise your oneness with everything that is. The only enemies that you have are those that lie within the ego state. Fear, superstition, selfishness, greed, avarice — these are the enemies of the higher state of mind. Replace them with love, kindness, tolerance, understanding, selflessness, peace and wisdom and you will find life will be so much more joyous, happy and rewarding.

Never forget, any of you, that the Great Spirit sees all, knows all and is all. Ultimately you cannot fail. The light of the spirit will shine through you. May I leave you all with my love and my blessings. I am with you always."

You are...

Lesser than no one,
As great as all,
Always heard,
Not neglected or overlooked,
Never forgotten,
Forever seen and known,
Eternally loved
and infinite.

....so why worry?

Visit the White Feather website
www.whitefeather.org.uk